A ROYAL TRADITION

THE QUEEN AND HER FAMILY IN SCOTLAND

Front Cover: *Queen Elizabeth at her Highlands home, Balmoral Castle.*
Back Cover: *Queen Elizabeth and Prince Philip dressed in the robes of the Order of the Thistle at the time of Her Majesty's Silver Jubilee Celebrations in Scotland in 1977.*

A ROYAL TRADITION

THE QUEEN AND HER FAMILY IN SCOTLAND

RODDY MARTINE

MAINSTREAM
PUBLISHING

First Published in 1986 by
MAINSTREAM PUBLISHING COMPANY (EDINBURGH) LTD.
7 Albany Street
Edinburgh EH1 3UG.

British Library Cataloguing in Publication Data

Martine, Roderick
    A royal tradition: the Queen and her family in Scotland.
    1. Elizabeth II, *Queen of Great Britain*
    2. Great Britain—Kings and rulers—Biography
    I. Title
    941.085'092'4   DA590

    ISBN 1-85158-018-2

Typeset in 12 point Van Dijck by Mainstream Publishing.
Printed by Collins, Glasgow, Great Britain.

'In my end is my beginning . . .'
Motto of Mary, Queen of Scots.

'How I wish we could travel about in this way,
and see all the wild spots in the Highlands.'
Entry from Queen Victoria's Journal, 1851.

CONTENTS

ACKNOWLEDGEMENTS

IT IS impossible to put together a book of this kind without consultation with a number of people far more informed on the subject than the author. That is, of course, where a training in journalism comes into play since all such exercises comprise the collating of thought from other peoples' minds and an individual interpretation. In particular I would like to thank my predecessors on *Scottish Field* for the useful coverage extended to the subject of Royalty since the magazine's inception in 1903. I would like to thank in particular Brian Reid of the Scottish Information Office for useful advice and statistics; Buckingham Palace Press Office; the Lyon Office, Edinburgh; the Army (Scotland) Information; *The Glasgow Herald*; *The Scotsman*; Camera Press; the Press Association; Andrew Large; Eric and Liz Thorburn, Zoe du Bois and the various private people who encouraged and advised me, but who wish to remain anonymous.

Acknowledgements for the Photographs used in this book:
Front Cover: Camera Press/Patrick Lichfield.
Back Cover: BBC Hulton Picture Library/Serge Lemoine.
Camera Press/Patrick Lichfield; Clapperton; Cunningham, Stewart; Glasgow Herald; HMSO; Kidd, Tom; Martine, Roddy; National Galleries of Scotland; Press Association; Reeve, Antonia; Robertson, Don; Scottish Field Library; Scottish Tourist Board; Thorburn, Eric.

INTRODUCTION

HISTORIANS will appraise the Reign of Queen Elizabeth II as the age when man first set foot on the moon, when satellites linked up the far corners of our universe both in sound and vision, when a British designed Concorde first flew the Atlantic at the speed of a bullet and when the computer microchip and laser science brought technology to unforeseen pinnacles of achievement.

In this book we follow the life of a young Princess who became Queen of England, Scotland and Wales, Northern Ireland and the Dominions at the age of twenty-five. Eight Prime Ministers have served her since the day of her Coronation on 2 June 1953. On 21 April 1986 she celebrated her 60th birthday.

This book sets out primarily to look at one aspect of the Queen's life. She descends from the Stewart monarchs of Scotland through both her father's Royal line and through her mother's noble Scottish family. It is through the Stewarts that she can trace her ancestry back to the ancient kings of Dalriada, some say to Gathelus, progenitor of the Scottish/Irish people, husband of Scota, daughter of Pharaoh Ramases II. Many of the qualities we see in her are inherently Scottish and, as has been the tradition with her immediate forebears, Scotland provides the one real escape from formality and State which the Royal Family can afford. Yet the ceremonial role of the monarch in Scottish life can be traced back over a thousand years. Scotland is thankful that the House of Windsor has neither forgotten nor neglected this tradition. This book is a tribute to Scotland's sixth Queen monarch and no apology is made for any Scottish bias which might be apparent.

Chapter One

THE TRIUMPH OF THE HOUSE OF WINDSOR

THE MOST poignant personal aspect in preparing this tribute to Her Majesty Queen Elizabeth II of the United Kingdom of Great Britain and of Northern Ireland and of Her Other Territories, Queen, Head of the Commonwealth, Defender of the Faith, has been an increased awareness of the passage of time. As a child I remember acutely the excitement which accompanied the arrival of a television set in my parents' home shortly prior to the Coronation in 1952. I regret to say that the actual Coronation ceremony had less impact on me than the miracle of being able to watch such a spectacle in black and white moving reproduction as it was actually taking place.

I do not nowadays recall much about the pageantry, although I do retain a mental picture of the Queen of Tonga, well over six feet tall, but this most probably is brought to mind by an unforgettable Noel Coward anecdote about her sitting beside her lunch, who was, as I vaguely remember, the Sultan of Kelantan. I wonder how much detail the Prince of Wales, who is approximately in my age range and who was physically present and spectating from the wings, recollects? But I do have in mind the broadcaster Richard Dimbleby's resonant voice in commentary and I was certainly impressed by the gold coach and the crowds in Pall Mall. As all the world knows the British excel at such occasions, even in the eyes of a child which take fantasy for granted.

It seems unthinkable now that thirty-four years have passed since that day. Unthinkable also that the Queen should have reached an age when most working women would be contemplating retirement with relish. Somehow, as with close friends and relations, you do not notice the passing of years. The familiarity of regular viewing makes you imagine that people whom you encounter at a certain age remain exactly the same forever. Only the punctuation of social ceremonies — births, marriages and deaths — reminds us that all things are transitory.

Probably this is what makes the role of the monarchy so significant to so many people. Royal births, marriages and deaths and great affairs of state provide a focus and continuity which people identify with their own lives. When Queen Elizabeth the Queen Mother visited the sites of German bombing in London during the Second World War, it reminded the British public that this was a battle which each and everyone was fighting for one another. When families gather together to watch the Queen deliver her annual televised message on Christmas Day, it brings a unity to the nation which is far divorced from politics and divisive forces. Inevitably there are detractors, but none can argue convincingly that the modern day role of the sovereign in the United Kingdom and Commonwealth is not unique in the history of the world. Pushing aside the debate as to whether or not the concept of monarchy anywhere is irrelevant and anachronistic in an age of egalitarian freedom and opportunity, one can pander to a more realistic discussion and analyse what the survival of the monarchy in this country has meant for the people of Britain.

The twentieth century has seen the collapse of monarchies throughout the world. When King Edward VII died in 1910, his funeral was attended by the German Emperor, the Kings of Spain, Greece, Denmark, Portugal, Norway, Belgium and Bulgaria, the Prince Consort of Holland and the Arch-Duke Ferdinand of Austria. Half of these ruling dynasties have survived, but after the 1914-18 War, nothing could ever be the same again. In Russia, Queen Victoria's granddaughter and her husband, the Tsarina and Tsar of Russia, were murdered by the Bolsheviks; in Germany, Queen Victoria's grandson, the Kaiser Wilhelm, initiated the first great world war and consequently lost his own Empire. In Britain such eminent figures as David Lloyd George were questioning the constitutional tradition of government, in particular the role of the House of Lords as early on as the first decade of the century.

It is therefore only to their credit that the British monarchy, through shrewd and subtle manoeuvering, has managed to survive the varied crises of this century and has gone on to boast, if it was want to do so, a far greater admiration and affection than it could possibly have claimed 100 years ago.

Constitutional problems such as the 1926 General Strike, the emergence of socialism as a political force in the United Kingdom and, in particular, the abdication of 1937, could all have contributed decisively to the demise of the monarchy, but the British are a rational people. Our roots and conciousness grow deep and we have tended to lean heavily towards patriarchal leadership without state control. Perhaps the Civil War which brought about the subsequent Cromwellian Commonwealth taught a useful historic lesson.

These factors aside, it is those individuals who occupy and create situations who must be appraised. The role of the sovereign is by definition and requirement, solitary and aloof. Yet the existence of a Royal Family, growing up and partaking of national life, is universally appealing and brings a surprising

The Royal procession at St Giles Cathedral, Edinburgh in 1977.

intimacy to the concept. The nation is justly proud of its first family.

But it is certainly within the last fifty years that this has emerged in full exposure. Photographs in newspapers and magazines, radio, the cinema and television have made the monarch and family familiar to every person in the land. Whereas King George IV's likeness, for example, would only have been instantly recognisable to the majority of his subjects from his official portraits, and only if any of them had been in a position to see one, the Princess of Wales is recognised the moment she enters a room, even when she might prefer to remain incognito.

There is no doubt that the media has made the Royal Family intimately well known throughout the world; at the same time, it has brought about an outrageous invasion into the privacy of individuals. And this is bound to create enormous pressures on the private lives of those within the Royal circle. The subjects of King Charles II and King George IV were relatively well acquainted with the indiscretions of the Royal bedchamber, but the illustrated life stories of the various mistresses concerned did not appear on the front pages of the popular press the morning after.

But times have changed since photographs of the uncrowned King Edward VIII wearing a bathing costume in the company of Mrs Ernest Simpson caused scandal and the proprietors of British newspapers were persuaded not to publish them as it was considered they could undermine the social stability of the nation. Nevertheless, there seems little which can be done and which has not been done since then to curb the insatiable desires of the world press to scrutinise the minutest detail of everyday Royal life in the hope of unearthing even the tiniest morsel of gossip. Consequently, minor revelations such as the one-time political affiliations of Princess Michael of Kent's father are exposed out of all proportion to the truth. And confronted with a continual barrage of nonsense and conjecture, the Queen has simply to grin and ignore it. Alternatively, her Press Office will usually issue a discreetly worded statement. But why should the Queen in her position be subject to such curiosity and bad manners?

The answer to some extent is that it is all part of the job. But it is also indicative that she does the job extremely well, and therefore all the world wants to know how and why she does things so well. Does any amount of wealth and position warrant such intrusion? Should anybody be expected to work such long hours under such a continual public spotlight? And with such a mass of publicity surrounding her public and private activities, is there not a continual risk to her security?

It comes down to the concept of duty at all times against all adversity, which underlines the current success of the British Royal Family, a notion somewhat old-fashioned and jingoistic by many standards, but one which nevertheless enabled King George V to see through the transitional constitutional changes of the 1920s and 1930s, which made it mandatory for his shy son King George VI to

The 4th Marquis of Aberdeen, King George VI and Queen Elizabeth in the Royal Enclosure at the Braemar Gathering.

take over the responsibility of state on his brother's abdication, and in turn qualified the young Queen Elizabeth II, supported by her mother, husband and grandmother, to take over from her father.

Writing on the subject of the abdication in 1938, Sir Compton Mackenzie made much of the emergent style adopted by the monarchy leading up to King Edward VIII. With regard to King George V, he comments, 'People did not want him to *do* anything. They wanted him to *be* something. That was his job . . . Set a good example in fact.' This is exactly what King George V had set out to achieve, and the 'good example' he passed on to his followers.

Mackenzie further pays tribute to that monarch: 'But the spectacle of the unfailing ability of King George V to adapt his behaviour to his people's ideal of a modern constitutional monarch, to provide neither more nor less than the amount of jam deemed necessary to flavour and lighten that huge, heavy roly-poly pudding of bourgeois sentiment, must not be allowed to obscure the gravity of the crisis that the progress of war (1914-1918) was seeming to the existence of royalty or the urgency of the question that progress was compelling every royal personage to ask himself. It would involve no exaggeration to assert that for the large number of European royalties, major and minor, belligerent and neutral, the result of the war was regarded exclusively from the standpoint of its effect on their own position in the future. In this respect, the British Royal Family was fortunate in being able to enjoy from a contemplation of the past some assurance that, provided they adapt themselves to the popular belief in their utility and the popular notion of how that utility should be demonstrated, they could rely with the utmost confidence on the profound affection of the British people for the monarchical institution — an affection which has survived the blow to the kingship dealt when Mary, Queen of Scots, was tried and executed for treason to a Queen of England whom a quarter of her subjects believed to be a bastard and usurper; the second blow to the kingship dealt when Charles I was tried and executed for treason to his own subjects; and the final blow to kingship which was dealt when James II and VII was abdicated and the legitimist line excluded from the succession; such an affection, however cruel sometimes, must be held cruel only to be kind to the monarchy.

'Nevertheless, whatever confidence might be placed in that affection for the institution of monarchy, King George, with the inestimably valuable help of his Consort, left nothing undone, not merely to relieve any possibility of straining that affection by even so much as being a few seconds late for a ceremony, but also by the gradual assumption of patriarchal dignity and authority to give a living force to the new aspect of the monarchy as the symbol of British unity the world over.'

Well put, and these then are the guidelines which have been followed by both King George V's second son and granddaughter with an almost religious fervour, though expertly understated. And within this concept and the accompanying codes of conduct, the association of a king and head of the Church of England with an American divorcee and his subsequent abdication in 1937, were considered by supporters of the system to be quite unforgivable. Not for nothing are King George VI and his Consort considered as the saviours of the British monarchy. Duty is all; self-sacrifice *is* necessary in the scheme of things. Hard rules, but again part of the job. Much has been written about the abdication, but for the purpose of further discussion, suffice it to quote the Duke of Windsor himself. 'I was to find out that tampering with tradition is fraught with trouble,' he confessed years later. 'The King, more than most men, is the prisoner of the past. The fault lay not in my stars, but in my genes,' he added somewhat dramatically. 'I was what I was.'

Whatever he considered himself to have been, he *had* impressed many in his years as Prince of Wales. The majority of his generation were stunned when he stepped aside from the sacred kingly path to marry the woman he loved. He undoubtedly believed that he was leading his nation into a more modern, free-thinking world. He was wrong. The nation was not yet ready, and where the ruling monarch is concerned is unlikely ever to be so. The outcome of King Edward VIII's selfishly motivated if otherwise romantic statement of love in which he rejected his birthright and duty was that his circumspect younger brother, who preferred country life and loathed speechifying, was forced into a role for which he and his Scottish wife had had no preparation. And a role which neither of them welcomed in the slightest.

'I never wanted this to happen,' the new King confided sadly to his cousin Lord Mountbatten. 'I'm quite unprepared for it . . . I've never seen a State paper. I'm only a naval officer. It's the only thing I know about.' Lord Mountbatten's response, of course, was that a naval training was a preparation to cope with anything.

I could not possibly at this juncture exclude Queen Mary's immaculate remark to the intransigent Prime Minister of the day: 'Well, Mr Baldwin, this is a pretty kettle of fish all right!' Queen Mary, the magnificent Consort, regal and distant, had suited immaculately the mood of her times. But history records that her emotions lay hidden behind that inscrutable majesty, and who could ever

King George VI and Queen Elizabeth at Ballater Station, 1948.

truly profess to know what her deepest feelings entertained in the drama which followed her husband's death. 'My second son,' she announced justly. 'He is the one making the sacrifice.' Formality not only governed public life, but exclusively dictated the conduct of the family. Queen Mary could say no more.

At the time of the Duke and Duchess of York's wedding in Westminster Abbey in 1923, there had seemed only the remotest possibility of their ever occupying the throne of Britain. The Prince of Wales was a conscientious young man, a glamorous figure popular with women. Songs were written about him and none doubted that sooner or later he would marry a suitable Royal bride.

For Royal she was expected to be. But when the York's engagement had been announced, the discussion regarding them centred on the break with precedent involved by a member of the Blood Royal marrying a commoner. The earls of Strathmore and Kinghorne descend from King Robert II of Scotland through his daughter Jean, so in common with most members of Scottish families, Lady Elizabeth Bowes-Lyon had Stewart blood in her veins. But the practice of nineteenth-century Royal dynasties had been to intermarry, and thus Queen Victoria's children and grandchildren had turned up in virtually every European Royal House. The consequences of in-breeding, however, had started to show. There was a cry from some quarters for good new healthy stock.

So the York's marriage itself heralded a new age in Royal unions. But the liaison with an American divorcee was going too far, too fast. Princess Elizabeth's betrothal to Prince Philip of Greece, on the other hand was entirely suitable. His father was a younger son of King George I of the Hellenes and grandson of King Christian IX of Denmark; his mother, Princess Alice of Battenberg, older sister of Lord Mountbatten, was eldest daughter of Prince Louis of Battenberg who during the 1914-18 war had renounced his German royal title to become 1st Marquess of Milford Haven. The stamp of approval was instant.

And more recently a future king has married another earl's daughter. Not without reason did Archbishop Runcie of Canterbury announce in St Paul's that 'Here is the stuff of which fairy tales are made'. Lady Diana Spencer could almost have sprung from a computer match-making service, although Royals most certainly do not resort to such agencies. Speculation on a suitable bride for the most eligible Prince in the world had given rise to some pretty wild conjectures, and for any couple to attempt the courting game under the full mobilisation of the world press is no pleasant experience.

Daughter of the 8th Earl Spencer and his former wife, The Hon Frances Shand-Kydd, Lady Diana Spencer had been brought up at Park House at Sandringham less than a mile from the Norfolk home so loved by King George V. So it can truly be said that she was 'the girl next door'. Lady Diana's maternal grandmother Ruth, Lady Fermoy, was lady-in-waiting to the Queen Mother, and ironically Mrs Shand-Kydd's own birth coincided with the death of King

Queen Elizabeth, consort to King George VI.

Members of the Australian Touring team photographed with King George VI and Queen Elizabeth at Balmoral in 1948.

George V at Sandringham. There is a story that Queen Mary, although distraught at the death of her husband, nonetheless remembered to ask after the health of Ruth Fermoy. Perhaps she sensed that this new-born child was to play a significant role in the future of 'The Firm', as King George V was want to call his family.

The wedding of Prince Charles Philip Arthur George Mountbatten-Windsor, 21st English Prince of Wales, Earl of Chester, Duke of Cornwall, Duke of Rothesay, Earl of Carrick and Baron Renfrew, Lord of the Isles and Great Steward of Scotland, Knight of the Most Noble Order of the Garter, Knight of the Most Noble Order of the Thistle, Great Master and Principal Knight Grand Cross of the Most Honourable Order of the Bath to Lady Diana Spencer has been both a domestic and public triumph. Once again nobody creates pageantry more spectacularly than the British and the wedding ceremony of this young couple captured the imagination of millions. It was a public relations exercise beyond comparison. The popularity of the Queen in her sixtieth year and her daughter-in-law in her twenty-fifth year has never been equalled.

With the births of Prince William in 1982 and Prince Henry in 1984, the glow of affection felt by a nation towards its first family has set firm. So it is entirely appropriate to conclude that despite the many turbulent upsets of the twentieth century, both international and domestic, the House of Windsor remains unruffled and intact, secure in the deep affection of its people, having lived up to their expectations, having shared the good times with the bad without complaint and uncompromisingly come out on top.

The Princess of Wales on a visit to Glasgow in 1983.

Chapter Two

AS SHE approaches the second half of her fourth decade as monarch and becomes eligible for a free bus pass, it is easy to be emotional and sycophantic about a woman who has uncomplainingly dedicated her whole life to the highest office of State in our land, a career which many might envy for the accompanying wealth and adulation, but others more realistically would deplore for the personal sacrifices involved. And after thirty-four years she has matured from the vulnerable young princess into the solemn, sometimes smiling, but always dignified, personage we see today. A professional woman who commands universal respect.

Whereas Prince Charles has been trained for his destiny from the moment he could walk — and no doubt the machinery is in hand to process Prince William in a similar fashion — there was no existing book of instruction for a young wife and mother to follow in 1952. This modern monarch of the 1980s is self-created, aided and advised by some formidable influences both within and close to the family circle.

It is true to say that in much the same way as Lord Melbourne counselled and to an extent cosseted the emergence of the young Queen Victoria, the elderly Sir Winston Churchill took the young Queen Elizabeth under his wing and, at times, seemed to have been utterly infatuated with her.

He had first encountered her at Balmoral when she was two years old, and writing to his wife Clementine his comments had a certain prophetic significance. 'There is no one here at all except the family, the household and Princess Elizabeth. The latter is a character. She has an air of authority and reflectiveness astonishing in an infant.'

What I find astonishing about the photograph of the little girl reproduced in this book on page 23, is that she is immediately recognisable — the stance and expression exactly as we know them today. Sir Winston's observations held true

The young Princess Elizabeth of York at Glamis Castle.

when over twenty years after that first encounter he enthused about her ability to cope with such great responsibilities at such a young age. But it is as though she has always possessed a certain self-assured nobility and, all considered, she has needed to change very little to meet the requirements of her role, despite the turbulent period of social transition through which she has lived. Is this, perhaps, what pre-destination is all about? Is seems incredible that she has never appeared to have put a foot wrong; that she has continued to project herself as exactly the person the majority of her people want her to be.

Harold Macmillan, that political grand master of the 1960s, later the 1st Earl of Stockton, once remarked to a member of the Royal Family that it was a pity that the Queen should so often look so solemn when she had such a superb sense of humour and fun. It seems the comment was passed on, as the Queen later instructed him herself that a Sovereign was expected to look serious — the people would hardly take her seriously if she was constantly grinning.

Since Sir Winston, seven prime ministers have served her country; counting

Princess Elizabeth at a fete in the grounds of Abergeldie Castle in 1933.

Sir Winston, six Conservative and two Labour. And both Labour Prime Ministers have not held back from expounding on how impressed they had been with her wealth of knowledge and common sense. Lord Home of the Hirsel, himself Prime Minister from 1963-64, had the following to say in his memoirs, *The Way the Wind Blows*: 'The Queen after twenty-five years of her reign (the book was published in 1976), knows almost every head of state and leader of government in foreign countries; while as Head of the Commonwealth she has an intimate knowledge of the leading political personalities and of their ways.

'Her experience is readily put at the disposal of the Prime Minister and is invaluable to him. Few realise the exacting nature of the work which it is necessary for the Sovereign to do, if she is to keep abreast of events all over the world which are of interest to her country. Her private secretaries are doubtless skilled in the selection and presentation of telegrams, but there remains a mass of facts and information which needs to be absorbed if Her Majesty is to meet

Princess Elizabeth at the age of 12 with Princess Margaret and Queen Elizabeth the Queen Mother at the Glasgow Exhibition in 1938.

Ministers of the Crown and foreign visitors on their own ground. The Queen, as I and my predecessors can readily testify, is always up to date and fully versed in the niceties of every national and international problem.'

One could be easily excused an expectation that the Queen lives in an ivory tower, but testimony from any person who has been in contact with her either socially or on matters of State confirms that she is probably one of the best informed and rational minds in the country.

Daily she receives minutes of Cabinet meetings, Ministerial memoranda and presentations, Foreign Office despatches, copies of *Hansard*, the record of day-to-day proceedings in the House of Commons, reports from her Ministers and governors-general in the Commonwealth. She reads the newspapers and, of course, there is a massive volume of personal mail. Courtiers are frequently astonished at just how much information she retains after a day's work; how up to the minute she is on the most diverse topics. But this is to be expected of her we tell ourselves; she is, in many ways, the protector of her peoples' interests. We do take her talents for granted, but then we seem surprised when she does things so very well.

Of course, the monarchy is far removed from the days of her ancestors when she could have ordered a head to be lopped off for insubordination. Queen Elizabeth 'reigns' but she does not 'rule'. But as Harold Wilson once testified, 'Any Prime Minister or other Minister who goes for an audience not having read some Cabinet papers that he is saving for the weekend may well feel at a disadvantage.'

What happens if the Queen does not agree with a suggested appointment? The monarch must at all times remain impartial and there is nothing constitutional she can do if she has a major objection. 'But I can always say that I would like some more information,' she once confided when asked this question, thereby introducing a not entirely subtle hint that all might not be as it should be.

You have to remember that the Queen is also head of fifty independent States. In this capacity, as Head of the Commonwealth, the Queen remains Sovereign of certain overseas territories without the stigma latterly associated with the British Empire. She remains Head of State and each government has equal constitutional rights which include the right to constitutionally reject the Sovereign. Her position, however, remains extraordinary and if she eccentrically chose, she is quite entitled, by law, to declare war, disband the armed forces, elevate every man and woman in the country to the peerage, pardon all prisoners and dismiss the civil service.

All acts of parliament are carried out in the name of the Sovereign, but the responsibilities for implementing them lie with Ministers dependent on a majority vote of confidence from the electorate. The Queen has a difficult course

The Marquis of Aberdeen, King George VI, Queen Elizabeth, Princess Margaret and Princess Elizabeth at Braemar.

to steer as the senior Civil Servant since she must at all times appear impartial and accept the actions of her elected Ministers and the policies of the government of the day. To reject them would be to oblige her Ministers to resign and in so doing to initiate a constitutional crisis.

To summarise, therefore, the Queen plays the role of a watchdog without bite but with the right to excercise wise council. At all times she has the right to be informed and to encourage or discourage should she see fit. Her strongest weapon is influence and it would be an unwise politician who chose to ignore such influence. While a politician can lose office or retire, the Sovereign preserves continuity of government as Head of State at all times, remaining the country's figurehead in the eyes of the world.

Although Britain has experienced an age of relative tranquillity during the reign of Queen Elizabeth, contrasting dramatically with wars and tragic confrontation elsewhere in the world, there have been moments of major disruption. Throughout the period from the Suez crisis in 1956 to the recent Falklands conflict, the immutable presence of the Sovereign afforded a calmness and confidence to the nation when politicians were loudly in search of political mileage. The murder of Earl Mountbatten of Burma and members of his family while on holiday in Ireland, the attempted kidnapping of Princess Anne in the Mall in 1974, the intruder in her bedroom at Buckingham Palace in 1982, all serve to emphasise the vulnerability of the monarchy. Yet nothing so far has stopped the Royal Family from doing what has come to be expected of them. Thankfully we no longer live in an age when it was deemed unsuitable for Queen Victoria's eldest son to visit the Marquess of Aberdeen's home, Haddo House, because he might be put into the position of having to meet the servants. Today the Queen and her family go walkabout in the streets of Britain in a fashion which creates nightmares for their security back-up, but wins them adulation from the populace. The modern Royal Family know the publicity value of being seen to disregard personal safety. The monarchy of today has to be seen to be in touch with the people and this means meeting as many of the ordinary folk about the place as possible.

It seems that they have also come to terms with the idea of assassination as a fact of life. If it happens, it happens. Unlike crossing a road and being knocked down by a car, assassination is not a prospect many of the rest of us thankfully have to consider in our lives, but we should not be unappreciative of what it means to those whom it might affect, especially when, from time to time, a warning shot is fired. But then who would want to hurt the Queen? Who would want to hurt the Pope, for that matter? The British really do not go in for that sort of thing. But the world we live in, whether we choose to ignore it or not, is full of twisted, unbalanced people and nothing is certain if you are considered public property.

Auberon Waugh, that scurrilous literary observer of humankind, in inimitable style recently analysed the Prince of Wales and concluded that he was, beyond question, a saint! No, his argument was not facetious; wittily put, his reasons were balanced and acute. Interestingly he did not attempt to label the Queen. Indeed, it was noticeable that he steered clear of the subject. I suspect that even he would find it difficult to elevate the Head of the Church of England much higher than she already is.

But one other verity he expounded is applicable to all the Royals. Nearly

Queen Elizabeth arriving at the Tercentenary Ball of the Royal Scots Dragoon Guards held in Edinburgh's Assembly Rooms.

everybody in the country, observed Waugh, reckons to know the Prince of Wales — possibly better than he knows himself. In Prince Charles' case this derives from every event of his life to the present day being closely scrutinised under the public gaze. Against this it is very difficult to have any secrets. But the Queen herself has achieved an aura, even if at times it comes over as slightly humourless and prudish. Whereas the heir to the throne is generally regarded as a nice chap and extremely approachable, the Queen is generally loved, admired, but is also relatively awe-inspiring, a state of grace which the Prince of Wales has yet to achieve, saint or otherwise.

I remember well the Tercentenary Ball of the Royal Company of Archers held in Edinburgh's Assembly Rooms in 1976. Scotland's aristocracy had dragged up every heirloom of family jewellery, bought, borrowed, stolen or rented they could find. Every wife or mistress of substance dazzled for the occasion, including the lovely Duchess of Buccleuch who wore the incredible Buccleuch emeralds around her waist as a belt. An onlooker commented that if everything on display that night was auctioned off, the sum of money raised would pay off the National Debt.

And then the Queen arrived, sparkling from head to toe. Nobody could fail to notice her jewels, and particularly her tiara, had been polished and consequently she looked almost ethereal. By comparison everybody else looked drab. This was the Queen of Scotland glittering among her own people at one of the grandest events of Scotland's social year.

Yet the Queen does not seek to upstage. It happens effortlessly, and behind it all there must be moments of intense strain and tiredness which she would never choose to show. Each year, indeed every week, there are numerous appearances and appointments to be attended to and after thirty-four years there must be moments of immense disenchantment.

Sir Michael Adeane, her private secretary until 1972, put it thus to the House of Commons Select Committee on the Civil List in 1971: 'All these engagements are enjoyable — and there are many who would welcome the opportunity of attending them. But for the Queen, who can never enjoy them with the freedom of a holidaymaker, the pleasure of attending them is bound to be tempered by the knowledge that somebody is looking at her all the time and that she is being continually photographed, filmed and televised as well. The strain of a long day in a provincial town, taking a lively interest in everything, saying a kind word here and asking a question there, always smiling and acknowledging cheers when driving in her car, sometimes for hours, has to be experienced to be properly appreciated.'

It would be nice to think that like her great-great grandmother, Queen Elizabeth keeps a diary so that one day, years from now, probably when all of us are long departed this mortal coil, historians can know exactly what she did think about it all. Does the impartiality of the monarch have to last beyond the grave? Possibly she might be able to tell our descendants how it was achieved and perpetuated — the mystic, that is. Beyond doubt there is a skilled working structure behind the public relations package which we are only partially aware of. Without question the British Royal Family is one of the best presented and intelligently marketed products of our time.

We are conscious of the Queen Mother's influence and, on reflection, one can identify how subtly that gloved hand has helped to guide the ship of state, particularly in the early days of her daughter's reign. Prince Philip's role must also not be underestimated. Then there are the many, many retainers for whom the continuance of the monarchy is synonymous with the breath of life. Not surprisingly, not a few of the immediate back-up team are Scots.

In 1977, Sir Martin Charteris, now 1st Baron Charteris of Amisfield, a grandson of the 11th Earl of Wemyss, retired as her Private Secretary. He had been appointed her Private Secretary in 1950 when she was Princess Elizabeth, so their relationship lasted for twenty-seven years, although he did not become Private Secretary to her as Queen until Sir Michael Adeane's retirement in 1972. Sir Martin was succeeded by Sir Philip Moore, who had taken up duties as Assistant Private Secretary in 1966. Sir Philip has proved an able administrator, but some people consider that he is more cautious and less innovatory than his predecessor. Sir Martin was always considered 'fun', but then a more established approach is quite appropriate as the Queen consolidates the achievements of her reign to date.

The role played by the Queen's ladies-in-waiting cannot be ignored. Assisting and accompanying the Sovereign on her public duties, they often act as her 'ears', bringing matters to her attention which others might dismiss as insignificant. The senior position, Mistress of the Robes, is held by the Duchess of Grafton, whose husband descends from King Charles II. Women of the Bedchamber include the Countess of Airlie, Princess Alexandra's sister-in-law, and whose husband is Lord Chamberlain. Another is the Hon Mary Morrison, daughter of Lord Margadale who has recently sold his family's fine home on the Island of Islay.

And another influential and unquestionably most difficult job is held by the Queen's Press Secretary, Michael Shea. He comes from East Lothian and writes books as a hobby under the name of Michael Sinclair. Press relations are critical since most journalists today are trained that if you cannot find a story, you invent one. A Press Officer must therefore strive for an informal relationship with the media which enables co-operation and at the same time allows him to enforce censorship when matters get out of hand. If it comes to a choice between the Royal Family and readership, most editors have no choice.

So we have been privileged to witness thirty-four years of evolvement

The Tercentenary Parade of the Royal Scots Dragoon Guards held in Holyrood Park.

—years of social and economic change when the British Empire finally divorced our tiny United Kingdom tucked into the corner of Europe — throughout which a young woman has worked steadfastly, adapting, but uncompromisingly, as she grew older, supporting and supported by her own immediate family in tune with the moods of a nation she was born to lead.

She must surely be the most travelled woman in the world. In her time she has played hostess to the great figures of the twentieth century — President Eisenhower, President de Gaulle, President Krushchev, President Kennedy, President Nixon, President Reagan, President Gorbachov, to mention but a few. Not for nothing was she described by the Japanese as 'Britain's most elegant saleswoman'.

Continually on the move, continually watched and always required to be attentive, at the same time expected to absorb so many facts and figures, the Queen must be possessed of the most immense reserves of strength and an all-embracing sense of humour. True or not, I have always liked the story of her once trying on a black dress at a fitting and asking her dresser Margaret McDonald to bring her out a large diamond clip. The Queen pinned it on the dress, casually threw a black mink stole over her shoulder and looking at herself in the mirror, she announced: 'If only somebody would invite me to something smart.'

Chapter Three

MARY, VICTORIA AND ELIZABETH

A NOTABLE feature of the Celtic law of tanistry is that succession does not require to pass outright to the next male relative in the line of a particular dynasty. With Scottish titles, deriving from their Celtic/Pictish origins, it has been common throughout history for a daughter to inherit when an immediate son and heir is not in existence. Right at the start, the original thrones of Alba and Pictland were merged through King Kenneth Macalpine's mother being heiress to the latter. The present Countess of Sutherland inherited her ancient Scottish earldom on the death of her uncle, the 5th Duke of Sutherland, whose English dukedom passed to a kinsman. The Countess of Mar, Lady Saltoun and Lady Sempill are three examples where a Scottish title and chiefship have passed to a female member of a family. Historically, therefore, the Scots have readily accepted the leadership of women, which might seem curious for such an otherwise chauvinistic nation.

Six women have inherited the throne of Scotland, but we can ignore Queen Mary of Orange and Queen Ann, as the former ruled her realms primarily through her Dutch husband, and the latter's only major impact on Scotland as such was to preside over the Act of Union (1707) which brought the Scottish parliament to England. Neither lady ever set foot on Scottish soil.

The tragic little Princess Margaret of Norway was barely four years old when she died at sea crossing from Bergen to Orkney to ascend her grandfather's throne in 1290, so it is therefore Mary, Queen of Scots, who first captures the imagination for the purpose of this book. She inherited the Scottish throne when six days old in 1542. Her father, King James V, had died brokenhearted after the battle of Solway Moss, defeated by his uncle, King Henry VIII of England. Scotland was in turmoil, appalled at the prospect of an English invasion. King Henry VIII was insisting that the baby Queen be married to his only son, and had the young prince, later King Edward VI of England, survived and had the match

Queen Elizabeth on Balmoral Estate at the time of her Silver Wedding in 1972.

Queen Elizabeth with some of her dogs at Balmoral.

taken place, how different the course of history would have been.

As it was, King James V's dying words themselves gave rise to conjecture. On hearing that his wife had given birth to a daughter, he is reported to have sighed and said with resignation, 'The Devil go with it. It came with a lass and it will go with a lass.' One assumes that he is thinking of the House of Stewart; the succession from King Robert Bruce's daughter Marjorie's marriage to Walter Fitz Stewart, 'The Steward', and an ignominious end with the birth of his daughter, powerless against her English great-uncle. I think it is a bit fanciful to suggest as some do that he foresaw the future — the barren death of Queen Ann, the arrival of the House of Hanover and the decline of the Stuart Jacobite cause which itself ended with a lass in the person of Prince Charles Edward's natural daughter, the Duchess of Albany.

But James undoubtedly underestimated his French wife and her supporters. Mary of Guise faced her bereavement with courage, but almost immediately there began what came to be called 'the rough wooing' where English forces under the Earl of Hertford ravaged southern Scotland with the purpose of persuading the Scots that a marriage between their child Queen and Edward of England would be entirely satisfactory. The consequence was that the Queen Mother kept her daughter safely in Stirling Castle and turned towards her home country for protection.

English pressure began to increase and in 1547, Hertford, now appointed Duke and Lord Protector Somerset, invaded for the third time, inflicting a major defeat on the Scots at the Battle of Pinkie. Realising that all about were intriguers and plotters, the Queen Mother decided that even Stirling Castle was not strong enough to preserve her daughter from certain of her noblemen's ambitions. The chosen refuge was a priory on Inchmahome, the 'Isle of St Colmoc', sometimes called the Isle of Rest. To this serene wooded hideaway in the Trossachs the five-year-old Queen was hurriedly taken, accompanied by four little girls of her own age for companionship — Mary Beaton, Mary Seton, Mary Carmichael and Mary Fleming. In July 1548 she was removed stealthily to Dumbarton Castle and then to France and to the French Court. Although safe from the design and manipulation due to her own country's political instability, Mary was to spend the following thirteen years in one of the most indulgent, immoral and debauched court circles in Europe, dominated by France's Italian Queen Catherine de Medici whose husband, King Henry II of France made little secret of his obsession with his mistress Diane de Poitiers.

The almond-eyed Mary was betrothed to the Dauphin Francois, two years her junior and whom she later married at the age of sixteen. While her daughter was safely out of the country, Mary of Guise took over the Regency of Scotland. It is sad to think that mother and daughter were to spend only a few months together in France when Mary was seven years old and that once the Queen Mother returned to Scotland they were never to see one another again.

Mary's schooling in France, however, was designed to equip her for her future. She studied Latin, Spanish, Italian and handwriting, and because there was no 'W' in the French language, the name 'Stewart' came to be spelled 'Stuart', which became the accepted spelling for her descendants thereafter. As the future Queen of France she was well indoctrinated into the Catholic religion by her maternal uncles and the ambitious Cardinal of Lorraine. Her wedding to Francois took place in the magnificent surroundings of the Cathedral of Notre Dame in Paris and in 1559, for all of one year, she became Queen of France.

Back in Scotland, meantime, all was far from well. This was a time when throughout Europe the new Protestant religion was exploding into violent confrontation with the Church of Rome. In Scotland, Lords of the Congregation (as they styled themselves) came into conflict with what they saw as a Catholic French government prompting the Queen Mother, supported by French troops, to pronounce unwisely that all Protestants were heretics. Fuelled by a sermon

An artist's impression of Queen Victoria and her family exploring the Highlands on shetland ponies.

preached by the reformer John Knox at Perth, a largely Protestant Scotland turned against the Queen Mother, rejecting her Regency and seeking protection, astonishingly enough, from the recently throned Queen Elizabeth I of England for so long as 'the marriage shall continue between the Queen of Scots and the French king'.

Roman Catholicism was formally abolished in Scotland and Mass was forbidden. Mary de Guise took refuge in the town of Leith, the seaport on the outskirts of Edinburgh, which she turned into a virtual fortress. Then in 1560, she died. The following year King Francis II of France also died. The nineteen-year-old Mary, Queen of Scots, and former Queen of France was on her own.

Imagine what it must have been like for a young widow, not yet twenty, educated as a devout Catholic in the libidinous surroundings of a Court society whose priority was the pursuit of pleasure. What further complicated Mary's position was that in the eyes of Catholic Europe, she was the rightful heir to the throne of England. Elizabeth Tudor, it was said, was the progeny of King Henry VIII's bigamous marriage to Anne Boleyn. Mary was descended from Henry VII of England through her father and grandmother and, therefore, the only legitimate claimant as far as the Catholic church was concerned. What served to incite her

Balmoral Castle, the Royal Family's Aberdeenshire home.

cousin Elizabeth even more was that, at the insistence of her father-in-law, Mary had assumed the Royal Arms of England and title of Queen of England.

The Scotland which welcomed its Queen in August 1561 was a drab, solemn place. Her arrival was premature and the welcome far from enthusiastic. Protestant Scotland was largely suspicious of the young Catholic Queen, an attitude encouraged by the all-powerful Lords of Congregation. It had not been Mary's decision to go to France, but the feeling ran strong that this was a stranger Queen come home to claim a birthright since she had run out of luck elsewhere. It says a lot for Mary therefore, that within two years she had won her people over without compromising her religion. In 1563 she made a Royal Progress through Scotland and was acclaimed by all despite determinedly maintaining her own right to worship as she pleased. There was trouble in the north east when she had to put down a Gordon uprising, but this whole adventure was the result of a misunderstanding on the part of the Earl of Huntly and not strictly a rebellion against Mary.

In England Elizabeth I had not taken a husband. In Scotland, the necessity to ensure the continuance of the Stuart dynasty became increasingly significant and what more suitable candidate could there have been than her own first cousin, Henry, Lord Darnley, whom the pretty young Queen described as 'the best

The little church at Crathie, near to Balmoral, where the Royal Family go to worship.

proportional long man we have seen'. Through their mutual grandmother, Margaret Tudor, he too had a claim to the throne of England. There were great celebrations and festivities at the Palace of Holyrood when this handsome couple were married in July 1565. But despite all its outward suitability, not least that it outraged the Queen of England, the marriage was a major mistake.

Darnley was the eldest son of Lady Margaret Douglas, Margaret Tudor's only daughter by the Earl of Angus, her second husband. Margaret Douglas was a great intriguer, but foremost a great survivor. In her early days at the Court of her uncle, Henry Tudor, she had frequently found herself acknowledged as the heir to his throne when that irrational king fell out with his various wives and their children. She was Catholic and after her marriage to the 4th Earl of Lennox, their home at Temple Newsam, five miles from the city of Leeds, became a centre for Catholic intrigue. From this background, Henry Darnley's character turned out to be weak, calculating and selfish, and what made matters more uncomfortable was that he was also personally ambitious, seeking Crown matrimonial status, ultimately aspiring to kingship. On the side he chose to lead a promiscuous lifestyle which could not but eventually be brought to the Queen's attention.

Mary bore her situation with dignity, but the jealousies which arose grew from Darnley's direction. He loathed first of all David Rizzio, an Italian musician who had accompanied the Queen from France, and whom she had appointed as her personal secretary in 1565. Darnley was not alone in this envy as the Queen had entrusted Rizzio with her total confidence whilst uncertain of the loyalties of many of the nobles who surrounded her. Naturally there was resentment. The matter climaxed when the Queen was six months pregnant. A group of Scottish nobles, including Darnley, Lords Lindsay and Ruthven and the Earl of Morton, burst into the room in which the Queen was having supper with other members of her Court, including the Countess of Argyll and David Rizzio. The unfortunate screaming Secretary was dragged to the floor and stabbed in front of the Queen's terrified eyes. There is a stain on the floor in the Palace of Holyrood to this day which is claimed to be that of David Rizzio's blood.

For Mary, such an unkindness was deeply painful and unforgivable. She could never bring herself to excuse Darnley, especially as he continued to behave in a boorish manner totally unsuitable for the Consort to the Queen of Scots. However, three and a half months after an experience which would have shaken any twenty-four-year-old expectant mother, a son was born at Edinburgh Castle.

It is impossible to know whether or not Mary was directly involved in the events that followed. It is certain that Darnley's continuing bad behaviour which led eventually to him contracting syphilis was discussed among her supporters and the conclusion was that it could no longer be tolerated.

On the night of 9 February 1567, the house in which Lord Darnley and his manservant were staying, at Kirk O' Field, close to the Palace in Edinburgh, was

Queen Victoria who re-discovered the Highlands of Scotland.

The Palace of Holyroodhouse, Edinburgh.

blown up with gunpowder. Incriminatingly Darnley's body was not found within the rubble of the house, but in a nearby garden. In fact, he had been strangled. Of course there were suspicions and accusations, notably against James Hepburn, 4th Earl of Bothwell, known to be an ardent admirer of the young Queen. It even came to a court case, but there was no proof, so Bothwell was acquitted. The matter might have rested there had Mary not three months later announced that she intended to marry Bothwell. This was yet another fatal error of judgement. If before it was believed that she knew nothing of her husband's murder, it was now widely upheld that she had been a conspirator from the start.

But there were also those who believed that there was another sort of sinister plot masterminded by Bothwell, who was generally disliked for a number of reasons, and that the Queen was being forced to marry him against her will. Bothwell was a rough man, considered uncouth by many, but nevertheless strong-minded and a man of action. After Francois and Henry Darnley, this could well have been what attracted Mary. She needed support and protection, but the argument that it was an imposed marriage could have something to do with the fact that Mary, separated from Darnley, was soon found to have become pregnant

Queen Elizabeth wearing the robes of the Order of the Thistle in 1984.

Queen Elizabeth and Prince Philip arrive at the Braemar Gathering in 1952.

again. In the following summer she miscarried of twins at Loch Leven Castle.

Mary's tragedy is that having triumphed at the start of her reign, winning the hearts of the Scottish people, she let it slip away, handing her enemies the very ammunition they required to bring her down. Knox and his followers seized their opportunity, lambasting the monarch's morals, and when Mary and Bothwell took refuge at Borthwick Castle, a sturdy keep not far from Dalkeith in Midlothian, a party of Scottish nobles rode out to arrest the couple. They escaped, but soon after, at a skirmish at Carberry Hill, Mary was taken prisoner and placed in Loch Leven Castle for safe keeping until she had agreed to sign papers of abdication in favour of her son, appointing a council of Regency to be headed by her own half-brother, James Stewart, Earl of Moray. Shortly afterwards the child James was crowned King of Scots at Stirling.

In the meantime Bothwell fled overseas into Scandinavia. He was arrested in Norway and for the following ten years held in chains at Dragsholm Castle in Denmark. Whether or not he would ever have tried to return to save Mary is pure conjecture as, despite his lion strength and courage, he eventually went mad and died in his cell far away from Scotland and Mary in 1578. In fact, his plight was brought to the public's attention not long ago when it was discovered that his decomposed body, still in chains, had never been removed to be buried and the personal plea of the present Queen Mother has happily rectified the situation.

Mary remained under lock and key at Loch Leven until an escape plot was hatched — in fact, two of her captor's sons, George and William Douglas, had become utterly infatuated by her. Once free, an army rallied to her support, but the forces of the Scottish Regency were somehow prepared. After defeat at the Battle of Langside, Mary fled south and took refuge at the Abbey of Dundrennan in Dumfriesshire. She concluded that she had two alternatives. The first, to return to France where, she accurately suspected, her welcome might not be over-enthusiastic. The second, to cross the Border into England where she would solicit aid from her cousin Elizabeth. With the same arrogance which was to bring down her grandson King Charles I, Mary believed in the divine right of monarchs and was convinced that Elizabeth could not fail to support a sister sovereign since she herself might any day find herself facing a similar problem. And it is true that Elizabeth of England was only too aware of Mary's dilemma. Elizabeth was also aware that Mary was also the greatest threat against her own position in a volatile England where Catholic plots took place around every corner. Elizabeth therefore kept her distance. Mary was placed again in captivity, this time for the remainder of her life, latterly at the Castle of Fotheringay, near Sheffield, sufficiently removed from both London and Scotland. The two women never met.

Mary was to spend the remaining nineteen years of her life in England. She had been in Scotland for only seven years. When she fled from her country she

The Lord Lyon King of Arms, Malcolm Innes of Edingight, CVO with (left to right) Islay Herald Don Pottinger, Unicorn Pursuivant Sir Crispin Agnew of Lochnaw, and the late Albany Herald, Sir Iain Moncreiffe of that Ilk.

The Prince of Wales photographed with Lady Diana Spencer at the time of their engagement. Witness the transformation into the Princess of Wales.

was twenty-six years old. And in her defence one must consider how many teenage girls could have taken on what she did and come through unscathed. In the seven years she lived in Scotland she had married twice, witnessed murder, quelled a major rising in the north east of her realm, given birth to a son, miscarried twins, been implicated in the murder of her husband, and had abdicated and been imprisoned for almost all of one of those years. They were indeed turbulent, brutal times, but seen popularly from today, Mary's story is full of excitement and romance and next to King Robert Bruce and Prince Charles Edward Stuart, she dominates the story of Scotland.

Thankfully, Mary's great-great-great-great-great-great-great grand-daughter, Princess Victoria of Kent and Strathearn, was able to reign successfully for sixty-four years over a far more civilised and ordered domain. And she also was a teenager when she took over the reigns of State, a year younger than her famous ancestor was when Mary had landed at Leith.

The opening lines of Queen Victoria's reign, 'I will be good', have come to be something of a cliche, but proved nonetheless prophetic. Her century saw the grand expansion of the British Empire and the Industrial Revolution which fundamentally changed the western world. Her private life was exemplary despite the curious innuendos concerning the friendship with John Brown, her manservant at Balmoral in her declining years. And it is true to say that unlike Mary she was enormously fortunate in her choice of Consort, her German cousin Prince Albert of Saxe-Coburg-Gotha.

Although she liked to claim that she was a Jacobite, in an historic context this would have been most unlikely. Her grandson, King George V, was once staying with the Duke of Atholl at the elegant Blair Castle in Perthshire and the two men began to discuss the Forty-Five Rebellion. 'Your ancestor was wrong,' insisted the King referring to Lord George Murray who had advised the Young Pretender to retreat from Derby. 'Had Charles Edward gone on from Derby, I should not have been King of England today.'

Victorian Scotland was powerfully influenced by the novels of Sir Walter Scott, who placed a strong picturesque bias on all things 'Highland'. The reasons which prompted Victoria's great-great grandfather, the Hanoverian King George II and his son, the Duke of Cumberland, to so ruthlessly crush the Highland clans could be overlooked when you considered all the noble sacrifice and sentiment embodied in the clansfolk's action when they rose up to fight for their Prince. Without examining the subject too closely, their values — loyalty and sacrifice —represented everything which the Victorian Empire held dear. The repercussions for those wretched people were gently overlooked in the quest for romantic ideology.

It was in the heart of this country which had witnessed so much bloodshed in the name of monarchy — the total devastation of the Highlands in the aftermath of the '45 — that Victoria found her greatest happiness and peace. At Balmoral her Albert landscaped the grounds and relocated roads to ensure their privacy. He even designed a Balmoral tartan. In the glorious surroundings of Upper Deeside their family would go hunting and shooting in much the same way as the Royal Family of today. Victoria's nephew, Kaiser Wilhelm of Germany, came to call and as a sign of favour was permitted to wear the Royal Stewart tartan. The Tsar of Russia and his family came to stay and it was an impressive family gathering — Prince Charles, later King Haakon of Denmark; Princess Maud, later Queen of Denmark and Princess Margaret of Connaught, later Crown Princess of Sweden. Empress Eugenie of France, descended herself from the Royal Stewart line through her mother's descent from the Duke of Berwick and Alva, principal grandee of Spain, came often to Scotland and when the Second Empire fell in 1871, the Queen offered her Abergeldie Castle on Deeside as a home.

When her beloved Prince Albert died in 1861 Victoria's world collapsed. Balmoral became his shrine. Nothing was to be changed, so that once the nightmare had ended and he returned as if he had never been away, all would be familiar. He did not return and his forest remained perfectly quiet; no heads shot by the prince were to be removed from the castle walls, and none added, unless exceptional. The Queen retreated into deepest mourning and was rarely to be seen in public. Two years later, she raised a memorial pyramid, a massive cairn standing thirty-five-feet high onto which, six years later, was placed a majestic statue. The inscription announced to all that it had been erected by the Prince's 'broken-hearted widow'.

As the years passed, Victoria began to revive her interest in life, but never entirely. She continued to wear black for the remainder of her reign. At Balmoral she came to rely more and more on the presence of a member of the estate staff, the son of a schoolteacher and small landowner, John Brown. In 1879 she titled him 'Personal Attendant and Page', endowing him with a servant of his own and building him a house, *Baile-na-Coile*, naturally giving rise to the wildest speculation from her other retainers and family members in the process. Onlookers were appalled at the outspoken and intimate manners of John Brown, but it may well be that this is exactly what had attracted the Queen to him in the first place. She knew that she had a servant whose loyalty and down-to-earth Scots common sense were beyond question or motive. When he died in 1883, the Queen mourned him as 'a trustworthy, discreet and straightforward man possessed of strong sense'. Had he lived today the media would almost certainly have had it entirely otherwise, but in all probability he was most likely nothing more nor less.

John Brown was buried at Crathie and Sir Joseph Boehm was commissioned to produce a life sized statue. The inscription on it reads: 'Friend more than Servant, Loyal, Truthful, Brave, Self less than Duty, even to the Grave'. The Queen was

The Honours of Scotland, the Crown, the Sceptre and the Sword of State.

not immune to the sentimentality so prevalent during her reign and to Balmoral's embarrassed factor, Dr Profeit, she presented a tie pin which incorporated a miniature of Brown, set in diamonds.

Victoria's life cannot be compared with Mary, but there were similarities between the two women in that they were both forced into positions of power at an early age and both inspired ardent loyalty, although Mary's waned after Darnley's murder and her entanglement with Bothwell, and Victoria's diminished as she moved into mourning for Prince Albert and away from public life. Both women relied heavily on the men closest to them, but were able to enforce their own wishes on those they loved when it suited them.

In 1953, Victoria's great-great granddaughter ascended the throne at the age of twenty-six. In her veins flows the same Scots blood which related both Victoria

Queen Elizabeth is accompanied by Lord Maclean of Duart on a visit to Bowmore on the Island of Islay.

and Mary back to the ancient dynasties of Scotland, the Houses of Stewart, of Bruce, of Dunkeld and of Alpin in the Kingdom of Dalriada, and before that to the High Kings of Ireland and beyond.

The late Sir Iain Moncreiffe of that Ilk, a most distinguished historian, derived enormous pleasure from working out the tangled paths of ancestry and was always pleased to point out that the Queen and Prince Philip together descend from Mary Queen of Scots no less than twenty times over through various cousin marriages within the ancestry of King George V and Queen Mary. Many other separate blood lines lead out into the Royal Families of Europe. As the descendant of Mary, there was undoubtedly a certain irony apparent when in 1960 the Queen addressed a special session of the General Assembly of the Church of Scotland held to celebrate the 400th anniversary of the Reformation in Scotland. 1987 marks the 400th anniversary of Mary's execution at Fotheringay and the suggestion has been put to the Post Office that they issue a commemorative stamp. Astonishingly it seems perfectly acceptable to put out stamps illustrated by the heads of British film stars, but to have Mary, Queen of Scots, on a stamp is even today considered controversial.

The Stewart line through Mary, Queen of Scots, is profoundly significant to the present monarchy, despite the split which took place over religion in the reign of Mary's great-grandson. Whereas the Tudors were descended from usurpers and conquerors, the line of Scotland's Ard Righs, violent, contentious people as they often were, poses far greater dignity of pedigree and legitimate descent. The Scots', and in particular the Highlanders', respect for their monarchs is underlined by the fact that they share a common history and lineage. On every occasion when a Stewart required the support of the clans and people of Scotland, the majority rallied without question.

Chapter Four

THE SCOTS AND THE MONARCHY

WHILST throughout history the Scots have often held their politicians in contempt, as a general course they have always remained loyal to their Sovereign. The reasons for this lie deep in Celto-Pictish culture and the particular brand of feudalism long ago adopted, but not forced upon the Scottish people. An intense 'tribe' obligation is central to this thesis. Inheritance and the land at a chiefly level have been fundamental throughout Scotland's development and it is only in the twentieth century that these concepts have begun to fall apart.

Much can be made of the cultural, distant racial differences of Highland and Lowland Scot; the former Celtic-Pictish-Viking, the latter Saxon-Norman. But the Scottish monarchy was a Celtic one and the clan system which developed was of a feudal kind — family organisations, if you like. The kind of feudalism adopted enabled the perpetuation of hundreds of tiny Celtic provincial states or clan territories, which together formed the Realm of Scotland. Each clan or 'tribe' had a chief and chieftains, but overall there was the High Chief or Ard Righ, who acted as the Law.

But there was another more fundamental factor. Writing on the Scottish clan system in 1938, that most distinguished of recent Lord Lyons, Sir Thomas Innes of Learney, put it thus: 'Hardly is there a Scot today who cannot in some line of ancestry connect himself with the Royal line of Fergus Mor McEarc, and claim as a kinsman Our Sovereign Lord, King George VI. This sense of kinship, the bond between the Ard Righ Albann and the great Peers and the Chiefs, between these and the duine-uasail, and between the latter and the clan, has had the most far-reaching effect upon our Scottish civilisation; for between the Peerage, the Houses of Chiefs and Chieftains, the Baronage, the Gudemen or less Lairds, and Tacksmen, it has been calculated that at the time of the Union (1707) there were (in a population of about a million) over ten thousand titled houses, each as proud and as nobly descended as any of the great Continental *noblesses*. Allowing for the

Queen Elizabeth 'nosing' whisky on a visit to Bowmore Distillery on the Island of Islay.

expansion of even the near circle of these houses and lines of Chieftains, it follows that about one person in each 45 were actually members of a 'titled or Chiefly house', and that about one-half of the Scottish nation consciously regarded themselves as members of the aristocracy. Such a proportion is unknown in any other nation, and the moral and social effect upon the Scottish nation has been incalcuable. Under the clan system, the lines of chiefs and chieftains were regarded as pegs upon which hung the glory of the whole race or sept, and their pedigree, preserved by the clan bards and historians, was treasured as the common pride of all the descendants of their line. But in this system no attempt was made to found a noble-caste, public-school class or snobbery of that description, and the younger members were expected by degrees to subside in an

Queen Elizabeth.

ever-extending pyramid into the duine-uasail and body of the clan, carrying with them through all ranks of the nation the pride and glory of lineage and achievement, and the sense of acknowledged blood-brotherhood upon either side, stretching throughout the whole gamut of the Caledonian social system.'

Sir Thomas expertly explained the underlying arrogance of all Scots, mischievously quoting Erasmus' observation of the Scots, that 'Their habit is to make great boast of their birth, and to claim kindred with the Royal Family'.

The Royal Family for most Highlanders in the seventeenth and eighteenth centuries meant the Stewarts. Highland memories are long and through the verbal tradition stories abounded of the great tragedy of Flodden and the death of the much loved King James IV. And there was Mary, Queen of Scots' much loved father, King James V, who liked to travel about his land disguised as a simple farmer, gaining himself the nickname of 'The Gudeman o' Ballengeich'.

When the Old and Young Pretenders made plans to regain their rightful throne from their Hanoverian cousins, it was to Scotland that they turned. For the Highland clans, many of whom remained Catholic, the rightful Stewart descendant was beyond question their acknowledged king. And so it was that both in 1715 and 1745 the Highland clans largely rose up to support James Stuart and his son Prince Charles Edward. And it became immediately clear to a government based in the south of England that they simply could not risk allowing the Highland chiefs to maintain what amounted to private armies to be used for such purposes. The clan system had to be broken. After Culloden, of course, it was, but the process continued through more subtle measures, and some not so subtle, such as the Clearances, where entire communities were driven from their crofting homes and traditional way of life to be replaced by sheep. Then such chiefs and landowners as remained began to send their sons south for education, to English public schools and to Europe, in many cases breaking the time-honoured contract between landlord and feudal tenant. A class system not dissimilar to that in England began to evolve, totally alien to the ancient clan concept. Life in the Highlands became more impersonal and more and more people moved away to the cities such as Edinburgh and Glasgow and many emigrated overseas to the New World.

But although the Scots have never been hesitant about bringing about change and although their politics are often radical and socialist, this is only to be expected. It is in their tradition and is, given the ancient structure of the clan society, deeply conservative. The Scots are proud and nationalistic, and these are inherited traits, which also embrace a special affection for the monarch. This might seem strange to an outsider, but again is part of their heritage.

Nationalism is also, of course, deeply ingrained. And it gives great pleasure to the Scottish conscience to be aware that the present monarchy of the United Kingdom descends primarily from the Scottish line. Reading the fourteenth-

Princes Street parade during the Queen's Coronation visit to Edinburgh 1953.

century document known as the Declaration of Arbroath which was sent by the Scottish barons to the Pope in Avignon requesting him to recognise Scotland's right to independence, one can not fail to sense the profound determination of the Scots to retain their identity: '. . . our folk lived under their protection free and undisturbed, until the masterful prince Edward, king of the English, father of him who reigns now, came in the guise of a friend and an ally with a hostile intent against our realm when it lacked a head, against a people who had no thought of ill or fraud, unused to the assaults of war. The wrongs he did among them, slaughter, violence, pillage, burning, prelates imprisoned, monasteries given to

Queen Elizabeth with schoolchildren in Perthshire.

The Prince of Wales in his uniform as Colonel-in-Chief of the Gordon Highlanders.

the flames, the inmates despoiled and slain, and these not all his lawless deeds, sparing neither age, sex, order of religion nor priesthood, only he who saw and suffered might recount or comprehend. From these unnumbered ills, with the aid of Him who heals the wounded and makes whole, we have been delivered by the strong arm of our prince and king, our lord Sir Robert, who, that he might free his people and his heritage from the hands of foes, a second Maccabeus as it were or a Joshua, endured cheerfully toil and weariness, hunger and peril. And he it is that by the providence of God, by rightful succession after our laws and customs, the which we will maintain even unto death, and by the dutiful consent and assent of every one of us, has been made our prince and king. Unto him, as the man through whom salvation has been wrought in our people, we are bound both of right and by his service rendered, and are resolved in whatever fortune to cleave, for the preservation of our liberty. Were he to abandone the enterprise begun, choosing to subject us or our kingdom to the king of the English or to the English

The crowds cheer their new Queen in Edinburgh in 1953.

The arrival of the Royal Coach at The Palace of Holyroodhouse in 1953.

people, we would strive to thrust him out forthwith as our enemy and the subverter of rights, his own and ours, and take for our king another who would suffice for our defence; for so long as an hundred remain alive we are minded never a whit to bow beneath the yoke of English dominion. It is not for glory, riches or honours that we fight; it is for liberty alone, the liberty which no good man relinquishes but with his life.

'Wherefore it is, revered Father and Lord, that we do pray your Holiness . . . look with a father's eye upon the sorrow and distress brought by the English upon us and on the church of God: be pleased to admonish and exhort the king of the English, whom it behoves to be content with what he has, seeing that of old England was wont to suffice seven kings or more, to leave us Scots in peace, dwelling in our poor Scotia, beyond which lies no place of habitation . . . If your Holiness take us not at our word, putting too easy a faith in what the English say, or haply cease not to favour them and we be confounded, the lives cut off, the sould sped, all the evil done by them in us and by us in them, we believe that the Most High must lay to your account. Wherefore we are and shall be in that wherein we are bound as sons of obedience to you His vicar ready to fulfil your pleasure in all things; and to Him as King and Judge supreme commit the defence

Prince Philip visiting Caithness Glass in Perthshire.

of our cause . . . Given at the monastry of Abirbrothoc in Scotland the sixth day of April in the year of grace on thousands three hunder and twenty in the fifteenth year of our aforesaid king.'

Eight years later King Edward III of England issued a document in response: 'We, Edward, by the grace of God king of England, lord of Ireland and duke of Aquitaine, give eternal greeting in the Lord to all who shall inspect the present letter. We, and certain of our predecessors as kings of England, have tried to assert rights of rule, dominion, or superiority over the realm of Scotland, and in consequence a grievous burden of wars has long afflicted the realms of England and Scotland; therefore, considering the killings, slaughters, crimes, destructions of churches, and ill innumerable which so often befell the inhabitants of each realm, by reason of these wars, and the advantages which would accrue to each kingdom, to their mutual gain, if they were joined by the stability of perpetual peace, and thus enjoyed greater security against the evil attempts of those within or without desiring to rebel or to attack them, we wish, and grant by the present letter, on behalf of ourselves, our heirs, and all our successors, with the common counsel, assent, and consent, of the prelates, magnates, earls, barons, and communities of our realm assembled in our parliament, that the realm of Scotland, defined by its true marches as they existed and were maintained in the time of Alexander, of worthy memory, the late king of Scotland, shall remain for ever to the eminent prince Lord Robert, by the grace of God the illustrious king of Scots, and to his heirs and successors, divided in all things from the realm of England, entire, free and quit, and without any objection, servitude, claim or demand. Any right in the realm of Scotland which we or our ancestors have sought in past times, in any manner, we renounce and surrender, by the present letter, to the king of Scotland and his heirs and successors. We remit utterly and entirely, on behalf of ourselves, our heirs, and our successors, all obligations, agreements and treaties undertaken in any way, with any of our predecessors, at

The Queen talking to old folk on her visit to Islay.

The Earl of Home, later to renounce his ancient Scottish title in order to become Prime Minister, presents Queen Elizabeth with the Sword of State of the Realm of Scotland in St Giles Cathedral in 1953.

any time, concerning the subjection of the realm of Scotland or its inhabitants, by any kings or inhabitants of the realm of Scotland, whether clerks or laymen. If any letters, charters, muniments, or instruments are found anywhere in future concerning obligations, agreements and treaties which have been made, let them be regarded as quashed, vain, null, and of no effect, and we wish them to be of no value or moment.

We have given full powers, and a special mandate, to our beloved and faithful Henry Percy our cousin, and William la Zouche of Ashby, and to each of them, by another letter patent of ours, to take an oath upon our soul for perpetually observing all these things fully, peacably, and faithfully. In testimony of this we have caused our letter patent to be made. York, 1 March, in the second year of our reign (1328).'

These two statements are fundamental to the whole course of Scottish history, The people of Scotland were rallied together almost in entirety for the first time to oppose a foe who sought to remove their independent sovereign rights. The unity — in general terms and under a Scottish monarch — lasted thereafter. Perhaps the thought is flippant, but it was more than fortunate that a Scottish king inherited the throne of England and not the other way around.

From the seventeenth century Scotland did not see a monarch for almost two hundred years. After Charles II, successive rulers stayed well clear until George IV paid his colourful visit in 1822. Thereafter, particularly after Victoria's exploratory foray in 1842, the House of Windsor began earnestly to claim back a neglected Scottish inheritance. A Scottish Queen in the person of Lady Elizabeth Bowes-Lyon also helped. Once, when approached at a reception by a South African who informed her that he detested the English, she replied, 'Oh I do so understand. You see I am Scottish.'

The Empire Exhibition held in Glasgow in 1938 and attended by the King and Queen saw crowds the like of which have never been seen before in Scotland. Although a number of Scots would deny that they showed any special enthusiasm during Queen Elizabeth's Silver Jubilee celebrations in Scotland, the streets of both Edinburgh and Glasgow were packed to capacity to witness the Royal processions.

Chapter Five

THE ROYAL HOUSEHOLD IN SCOTLAND

PAGEANTRY not only focuses our attention on great affairs of State it reminds us of our heritage. The rituals and the individuals taking part represent great moments from our history which many of us are unaware of.

As the crowds cheered and waved while the Queen passed through the streets of Edinburgh and Glasgow during her Scottish Silver Jubilee celebrations in 1977 there must have been those who wondered who the haughty looking individuals in the other carriages were and what they were doing there. In fact, each individual signified a historic office. Their presence in those parades reminded us of the past, showing that Scottish pageantry and the monarchy have survived with all its unique national features since the days of King Robert Bruce.

In the first carriage, the Balmoral Landau (in which Queen Victoria crossed the Alps with John Brown), accompanied by two pursuivants of the Lyon Court, were the two Hereditary Standard Bearers of Scotland, the Earls of Dundee and Lauderdale. The Earl of Dundee's ancestor, Alexander Schyrmeschur, son of Colin, son of Carun, was confirmed the perilous, but honourable privilege of carrying the king's banner in war, and the office of Constable of the Castle of Dundee. These offices were awarded to him on behalf of the crown and realm of Scotland by William Wallace, Guardian of the Kingdom of Scotland, and Robert Bruce. The unfortunate Alexander was taken prisoner of war and hanged at Newcastle-upon-Tyne by the express orders of Edward I of England, but the office of banner bearer remained hereditary. In the seventeenth century, the Duke of Lauderdale, who was Secretary of State for Charles II, acquired the banner-bearer's office for himself, but after a complicated court case in recent years, a compromise was reached permitting the earls of Dundee to once again carry the Royal Banner of Scotland on State occasions, and the earls of Lauderdale to carry the Saltire Banner of Scotland instead.

In the fourth carriage of those processions sat the Lord High Commissioner to

Queen Elizabeth's Coronation visit to Edinburgh 1953.

the General Assembly of the Church of Scotland. This appointment is made annually by the Crown and the Commissioner represents the monarch, is styled Your Grace, and takes precedence over all except the monarch, including other

The Royal Carriage on the Mound, Edinburgh during the Queen's Coronation visit to Scotland 1953.

The Queen and Prince Philip travelling along Princes Street during the Queen's Coronation visit to Edinburgh in 1953.

members of the Royal Family. The Lord High Commissioner takes up residence at Holyrood Palace during the annual General Assembly and is the Queen's representative. In recent years the Commissioners have included Lord Ross, the Earl of Elgin, and Lord Maclean of Duart. In the same carriage travelled the Purse Bearer, whose purse contains the Royal Commission, and the Secretary of State for Scotland, a government appointment. Until recently the Lord Chamberlain of the Realm was Lord Maclean of Duart, 27th Chief of Clan Maclean, whose spectacular family home is Duart Castle on the Island of Mull. 'Chips' Maclean was formerly Chief Scout of the Commonwealth and has written a story book for children among his other achievements. As Lord Chamberlain he organised both the weddings of Princess Anne and the Prince of Wales, and the funerals of the Duke of Windsor and Lord Mountbatten. In his retirement he has been appointed Chief Steward of Hampton Court Palace, which was built by Cardinal Wolsey and acquired by King Henry VIII. Lord Maclean was succeeded as Lord Chamberlain in 1984 by David Ogilvy, 13th Earl of Airlie, following in the footsteps of his father the 12th Earl, who was in that office for Queen Elizabeth, later the Queen Mother. Lord Airlie is chief of clan Ogilvy and comes from an ancient Scottish family whose home is Cortachy Castle, Kirriemuir.

The Lord Chamberlain attends the Queen on ceremonial occasions at Court, where he is required to walk backwards carrying his white stave of office. He organises State visits, garden parties and investitures. He is the official arbiter on protocol, precedence and the details of stars and ribbons worn on such occasions.

In 1977, the Lord Chamberlain shared his Semi-State Laundau carriage with two other clan chiefs. The 12th Duke of Argyll, Chief of Clan Campbell, carried the baton of Hereditary Master of the Royal Household in Scotland, an office held by his family since 1464, but created a hereditary post by King James V in 1528 and confirmed by Queen Victoria. His office is not to be confused with that of the Duke of Hamilton, who is Hereditary Keeper of the Palace of Holyroodhouse. The other chief present was the 24th Earl of Erroll, who inherited the chiefship and title through his mother. The Errolls are Hereditary Lord High Constables of Scotland originating from their ancestor Sir Gilbert de Haye who was awarded the honour by Robert Bruce in 1314 after the Battle of Bannockburn. The Lord High Constable, who carries a ceremonial baton, is responsible at all times for the safety of the Sovereign's person; in effect, he is her ceremonial bodyguard.

Stewart kings rewarded loyal retainers with hereditary offices relating to great castles of the Realm. The Macleans, for example, were confirmed Hereditary Keepers of Dunconnel Castle in the Isles of Sea in 1495. Although this honour was subsequently withdrawn from them 200 years later, Sir Fitzroy Maclean of Dunconnel, a descendent of the 11th Hereditory keeper successfully petitioned the Court of the Lord Lyon in 1980 to re-claim the distinction for his family.

Dunstaffnage Castle in Argyll is held for the monarch by the Duke of Argyll through his Hereditary Captain, Campbell of Dunstaffnage. Edinburgh Castle is held by a governor, traditionally the General Officer Commanding Scotland. Hereditary keeper of the Palace of Holyroodhouse is the 15th Duke of Hamilton and Brandon, Premier Duke of Scotland. This office was bestowed on his

Members of the Household Cavalry in Glasgow en route for George Square in 1977.

Queen Elizabeth with the Royal Company of Archers at Holyrood Palace.

Queen Elizabeth and Prince Philip during the Queen's Silver Jubilee visit to Edinburgh in 1977.

Queen Elizabeth addressing the General Assembly of the Church of Scotland in 1977.

ancestor, the 1st Duke of Hamilton in 1646, and successive keepers appoint their Bailie who presides over the High Constables of Holyrood, top hatted, plumed gentlemen who turn out as Guards of Honour for the Sovereign when required.

The Palace of Falkland in Fife, much beloved by King James VI, has Ninian Crichton-Stuart as Hereditary keeper, although the property is now maintained by the National Trust for Scotland which acts as Deputy keeper. Then there is Stirling Castle which has seen so much of Scotland's history enacted within and in front of its walls. The Lords Erskine, later the Earls of Mar have been Hereditary keepers since the 16th century, and the present Earl of Mar and Kellie occupies the office which was restored to the 14th Earl by King George V in 1923.

Finally, there is Rothesay Castle on the Isle of Bute where, as one would expect, the 6th Marquis of Bute is keeper as well as being Hereditary Sheriff of Bute. The appointment of the present Marquis' ancestor was made by King James VI in 1498.

Other great offices do not specifically relate to pageantry or State occasion. For example, the Dean of the Chapel Royal, the oldest non-ecclesiastical office in Scotland which dates back to King Alexander I in 1120. There are the Royal Historiographer and the Royal Astronomer, the latter a post which derives from the founding of the Astronomical Institution of Edinburgh at the end of the 18th century. King George IV gave Royal status to the Observatory which was built in Edinburgh in 1818, and when the Regius Chair of Astronomy established at Edinburgh University in 1786 was amalgamated with the Royal Observatory, the directorship and professorship combined to take on the role of Her Majesty's Astronomer Royal for Scotland.

In 1703, Queen Anne established the office of Painter and Limner. Sir David Wilkie held the appointment in 1823, as did Sir David Young Cameron in 1933. The present holder of this distinction is the elfin David Donaldson RSA, one of Scotland's most innovative and excellent portrait painters.

There are other hereditary posts too. The Setons are Hereditary Armour Bearers and the Carmichael-Anstruthers are Grand Carvers of Scotland. These great Offices of the Household are called upon to be fulfilled when the ceremonial function demands it. The most senior office of all is that of Hereditary Great Steward of Scotland and that is the office proudly borne by the heir to the throne.

These dignitaries might understandably seem anachronistic and privileged to many onlookers but their presence is part of the uniqueness of Scottish life. Each and every civilisation needs structure and tradition and, in each generation, the presence of representatives of families who, like the Royal Family itself, have played critical roles in the volatile shaping of our nation gives a sense of stability and continuity to our way of life.

Chapter Six

THE SCOTTISH REGALIA

EACH YEAR visitors to Edinburgh Castle exclaim with delight when they visit the Crown Room and see the Scottish Regalia on display — the ancient Scottish crown, the sceptre and sword of state. The Scottish Regalia, however, are only there to be admired because of an extraordinary escapade which took place over three hundred years ago.

In 1651, Lord Protector Cromwell was marching on Scotland after the Scots had audaciously crowned Charles II king at Scone. The Covenanting party who had thus acknowledged Charles came to the conclusion that if Cromwell seized Edinburgh Castle, the Honours of Scotland would be among the first things he would destroy. Parliament therefore ordered that they be taken to a place of safety, and Dunottar Castle, a stronghold on an almost inaccessible promontory on the coast of Kincardineshire, was chosen as a safe location. The various items were taken there, where the governor, George Ogilvie of Barras, took the responsibility of hiding them. But Cromwell soon discovered what had happened and sent a force north to retrieve them. The castle was put to siege and after a time it became apparent that the defenders would not be able to carry on indefinitely. A plan to save the Honours had to be hatched immediately.

Now, it transpired that the governor's wife was a friend of a Mrs Christian Granger, the wife of the Rev James Granger, minister of the neighbouring parish church of Kinneff. The two women somehow managed to communicate and it was arranged that the Granger's servant girl would go frequently along the cliffs beneath the castle battlements to gather flowers, 'dulse and tangles'. She went so regularly that the siege troops became friendly with her and became quite used to seeing her with her basket. Eventually it was decided that it was time to act. One day the Honours were lowered over the cliff to the servant girl and she placed them in her basket, covering them with seaweed. The Sword of State had to be snapped in two and to this day you can see where it has been joined up again. The girl coolly returned to her mistress, passing through the Cromwellian troops who paid her little attention.

For a few days the Regalia was hidden at the bottom of the minister's bed in the manse. They were then taken to the church. In case something should happen to him Mr Granger wrote a letter to the Countess Marischal. He told her how at night he had raised up the pavement stone in front of the pulpit and dug a hole. Into this he placed the Crown and Sceptre. Having filled up the hole and replaced the stone, he buried the sword in the west end of the church, between two pews.

In June Dunnottar Castle fell, Ogilvy deciding that they could no longer hold out. One of the conditions of surrender was that the Regalia should be handed over. When the Governor refused to do so, he and his wife were thrown into a dungeon, where they died. This act of valour deserves more publicity than it has been given in the annals of Scotland.

As it transpired, the Regalia remained hidden at Kineff for nine years until the restoration of King Charles II in 1660. Once more they were returned to Edinburgh Castle and in a clause of the Act of Union in 1707, it states that they must continue to remain 'in that part of the United Kingdome now called Scotland, and that they shall remain in all tyme coming, notwithstanding of the Union'.

The responsibility for the Regalia fell to the Commissioners of the Treasury who decided that they should be locked up in an oak chest and walled up in the Crown Room of the Castle. For more than a hundred years they were forgotten, even though the Crown Room was opened up in 1794 under a Royal Warrant to search for some missing papers. The Commissioners suspected that the chest contained the Regalia, but they could not find the key and had not the authority to force the lock.

It was Sir Walter Scott who eventually persuaded the Prince Regent, later George IV, to give him a warrant to open the chest. Sir Walter described the scene in his inimitable way: 'The chest seemed to return a hollow and empty sound to the strokes of the hammer, and even those whose expectations had been most sanguine felt at the moment the probability of disappointment, and could not but be sensible that, should the result of the search confirm their forebodings, it would only serve to show that a national affront and injury had been sustained, for which it might be difficult, or rather impossible, to obtain any redress. The joy was therefore extreme when, the ponderous lid of the chest being forced open, at the expense of some time and labour, the Regalia were discovered lying at the bottom covered with linen cloths, exactly as they had been left in the year 1707 . . .'.

In the Coronation year of Elizabeth, the Honours of Scotland were taken out of Edinburgh Castle and borne before the Queen 'in full sight of the people' for the first time since 1822. They were carried on a velvet cushion by the Lord Lyon King of Arms, High Sennachie to the Royal line, Minister of the Crown, of the Kingdom, Judge and Master of Ceremonial. He is Scotland's leading authority on genealogy and heraldry, and in days of old, at all Coronations, the Lord Lyon would recite in Gaelic the Royal genealogies, the lineage being taken back to King Fergus. Coats of Arms, the science of Armoury, or Heraldry, if you prefer, as a system of identification was evolved in the twelfth century. In order to prevent mistakes in battle through misuse or fraud in sealing deeds, the Monarch had to arrange for heraldry to be controlled, and, similarly, the settlement of disputes over succession, inheritance, and so on. The business was relegated to the Royal Sennachie of Celtic Scotland, the chief genealogist, who then became the Lord Lyon King of Arms. This 'awesome' office represents the Monarch and Lyon wears a tabard of the Royal Arms.

Only arms granted by the Lyon Office are admissible. In 1592 and 1672, the Scottish Parliament forebade the use of arms not so confirmed and established the Public Register of All Arms and Bearings in Scotland, which is kept in the Court of the Lord Lyon at Register House in Edinburgh. Under Act of Parliament it is unlawful to use any arms which have not been matriculated in that Register, or to use the registered arms of any person of whom you are not the lawful heir.

The Lord Lyon's jurisdiction comprehends 'all badges and cognisances whatsoever borne and used' and his duties have particular reference to family and community genealogies, the armorial insignia of the leaders holding high military or civil jurisdiction throughout the realm of Scotland — thus the chiefs of clans

The Palace of Holyroodhouse, Edinburgh.

and, among other things, the patenting of tartan. The present Lord Lyon is the portly, jovial Malcolm Innes of Edingight, Baron of Yeochrie, Companion of the Royal Victorian Order, and Writer to the Signet, a son of the most celebrated Lyon of this century, Sir Thomas Innes of Learney, remembered for his high-pitched voice and the Doric inflections abandoned by so many of his fellow Scots in favour of English public-school education. Malcolm Innes himself served as Lyon Clerk from 1966 until 1981, when he took over office from Sir James Monteith-Grant.

There are some colourful characters in the Lyon Court. The Albany and Rothesay Heralds take their titles from the Royal Dukedoms in Scotland. Marchmont Herald derives from the Royal Castle of Marchmont in Roxburgh in 1438 and nobody is quite certain about the Islay Herald, but he has been around since 1493. There are Pursuivants Ormond and Carrick, and the colourfully titled Unicorn Pursuivant originates from the Unicorn in the Royal Arms. It is not uncommon in the Lyon Office to overhear a conversation which begins, 'Hello, is that Unicorn? Lyon here.' The heralds wear the Queen's own coat-of-arms as marshalled in Scotland; the Lyon of Scotland quartered first and fourth; the leopards of England second; and the harp of Ireland third. Between the wars it was necessary to raise a public subscription in Glasgow to provide tabards in the correct Scottish form instead of ones with the English leopard first and fourth.

The greatest honour in Scottish life is to be made a Knight of the Most Ancient and Most Noble Order of the Thistle. Revived in 1687 by King James VII and II, the Order is said to have arisen in the mists of antiquity. James's daughter re-established the Order in 1703, and it was introduced again by King George VI, possibly as much a sign of affection for his Scottish wife as anything else. One of the first knights invested by King George was his father-in-law, the Earl of Strathmore. The Most Ancient and Most Noble Order of the Thistle is the Scottish equivalent of the Order of the Garter. The Order was formerly assigned to the Chapel Royal at Holyrood and consisted of the Sovereign and twelve knights. The number was increased to sixteen in 1821 and, in 1911, the splendid Thistle Chapel at the south-east corner of St Giles Cathedral was completed by Sir Robert Lorimer and dedicated.

The Insignia of the Thistle consists of (1) the Star, made up of a St Andrew's Cross of silver embroidery with rays emanating between the points of the cross; in the centre upon a field of gold, a Thistle of green, heightened with gold, and surrounded by a circle of green, having thereon the motto in letters of gold, *Nemo me impune lacessit*. The Star is worn affixed to the left breast. (2) The Collar is of gold and consists of thistles intermingled with sprigs of rue. There is a pendant from the centre, the St Andrew of gold enamelled with the gown green and the surcoat purple, bearing before him the cross enamelled white, and having round the image rays of gold going out from it in the form of a glory. (3) The Mantle is of green velvet bound with taffeta and tied with tassels of green and gold; on the left shoulder is a representation of the Star of the Order. (4) The Badge (of gold enamelled) has on one side the image of St Andrew with the cross before, enamelled as above described or cut in stone, and on the back enamelled a Thistle, gold and green, the flower reddish, with the before-mentioned motto round it, the Thistle on an enamelled green ground. It is worn attached to a dark green ribbon passing over the left shoulder and resting on the right hip. (5) The Hat is of black velvet, ornamented with osprey plumes.

At death, the Badge and Star are delivered up to the Sovereign by the Knight's nearest male relative, the Collar (with pendant Badge) being returned to the Central Chancery, which is in the Lyon Office.

Current Knights of the Thistle are Lord Home of the Hirsel, who is Chancellor, the Earls of Elgin, Haddington, Wemyss, Dalhousie, Airlie and Selkirk, the Duke of Buccleuch, Lord Maclean of Duart, Lord MacFadzean, Lord Clydesmuir, Viscount Muirshiell, Lord Thomson of Monifieth, the Hon Lord Cameron, Sir Donald Cameron of Locheil and Lord MacLehose of Berch.

The Royal Company of Archers, the Queen's Bodyguard in Scotland, was founded as firearms were introduced and archery as a 'war weapon' disappeared. Over three hundred years old, the bodyguard comprises 'an influential body of noblemen and country gentlemen, for the purpose of encouraging the noble and useful recreation of archery'. Nowadays only about one-tenth of the 400 members actually shoot for the series of annual prizes which have been contested over the centuries, but the rest of them are called upon to turn up in their green uniforms and eagle feathered Balmoral bonnets (soft for shooting, stiffened for ceremonial appearances) at Holyrood Garden Parties and at Thistle ceremonies.

Ordinary Archers wear one eagle feather, officers two and the Captain General three. The first Captain General was John, Marquis of Atholl. Since then the heads of many noble Scottish families have held the post. To become an Archer you have to be of Scottish descent, to own land in Scotland or to have served in a Scottish Regiment. Archery competitions are held in public places like Edinburgh's Meadows and the Musselburgh racecourse, no doubt causing considerable amusement and interest to passers-by. The oldest archery competition recorded is the Musselburgh Arrow in 1603. It is also the oldest sporting trophy of any sort in the United Kingdom. Other competitions take place at Peebles, Selkirk and Montrose and usually the prizes are silver arrows to which are added each year medallions naming the winner. Close to Edinburgh University is Archer's Hall, where the company held their first Mess dinner in 1777. Archer's Hall was built 100 years after the formation of the Company and until then members who met regularly to shoot had dined afterwards at city taverns.

The present site was chosen because of its proximity to their principal shooting ground, the Meadows, and the building is attractive early Georgian with some Victorian additions. In the entrance hall are displayed several old uniforms — one of 1777 in tartan — and samples of old Mess coats and Court dress. Also on show is a redendo dating back to when Queen Anne gave the company their first Royal Charter, for which they had to render yearly one pair of barbed arrows — if requested. The redendo, as such, is three arrows on a velvet cushion and it was presented to King Edward VII in 1905 and handed back to them by King George VI as a memento of his visit. On the staircase wall leading to the dining hall are several bows, one of yew and another, a cumbrous relic of Flodden. This curious body or wealthy of well-connected individuals, the Royal Company of Archers, although nowadays of a primarily social nature, provides a colourful addition to every Royal visit to Scotland.

Chapter Seven

SCOTTISH BLOOD — THE RELATIVES OF THE HOUSE OF WINDSOR

ROYAL MARRIAGES in the past often took place for reasons far removed from compatability or love and it is surprising how many of them came to work successfully. The guiding instinct, of course, was duty. But the further away someone was from the Throne the more opportunity they had to lead their own life and to make their own choices.

The marriage of the eldest son of the 8th Duke of Argyll to Queen Victoria's fourth daughter, Princess Louise, in 1871 did not meet with universal approval. Many members of the British and German Royal families frowned on the match between a Princess and a subject, even though both could claim descent from King James I of Scotland. Surprisingly, Queen Victoria, who had been friendly with the Argyll family since her first adventure into Scotland, rose to her daughter's defence, saying, 'Small foreign princes are very unpopular here.'

Princess Louise was considered the most beautiful of Queen Victoria's daughters. Certainly her portrait shows her to have a serene and wistful quality which was much admired by that generation. Her marriage to John Campbell, Marquess of Lorne, was not a great success, but thier unhappiness was never visible in public. In 1878 he became Governor-General of Canada and the Princess suffered an appalling sleigh accident, being dragged along the snow by her hair and losing an ear in the process. Whether or not it was a result of this or her general discontent, Louise acquired the reputation of being bad-tempered and of having a vicious tongue. She was not particularly popular with other members of her family as a result.

Yet she was obviously very talented. She became an accomplished sculptress and an example of her work is the memorial to Prince Henry of Battenberg in Whippingham Church, near Cowes. There is also her statue of Queen Victoria at Kensington Palace. In addition, she wrote articles for magazines under the name of Myra Fontenoy and took a special interest in the education of women. Lord

Lorne, who succeeded his father as Duke in 1900, wrote fiction, encouraging the Scottish composer Hamish McCunn by writing the libretto to his music for an opera. He wrote several books on Canada and a biography of Lord Palmerston. In 1892 he was appointed Governor and Constable of Windsor Castle, an office he held until his death in 1914. Childless, Princess Louise lived on until 1939.

Four years before the marriage of Princess Louise, Marchioness of Lorne, in 1871, there had been born another Princess Louise, the eldest daughter of King Edward VII and Queen Alexandra, when they were Prince and Princess of Wales. In 1899, this Princess Louise married Alexander Duff — Lord MacDuff, son of the 5th Earl of Fife. He was a rich landowner eighteen years older than his bride and Queen Victoria created him 1st Duke of Fife. The couple had two daughters, Princess Alexandra, who married Prince Arthur of Connaught, and Princess Maud, who married the 11th Earl of Southesk. As the eldest daughter of a king, Princess Louise was granted the title of Princess Royal in 1905. The Duke died in Egypt in 1912 and the Dukedom devolved by special remainder to his eldest daughter. The Princess Royal lived until 1931. The Dukedom of Fife next devolved on to the son of Prince Arthur and Princess Arthur of Connaught. He took the title of Earl of MacDuff, succeeding to his grandfather's Dukedom in 1942.

The younger daughter of the Duke of Connaught and Strathearn, Queen Victoria's third son, was christened Princess Patricia in 1886. At the age of thirty-three she was finally able to marry the husband of her choice, the Hon Alexander Ramsay, a son of the 13th Earl of Dalhousie. Two days before her wedding she asked to relinquish her royal style and title and was thereafter known as Lady Patricia Ramsay. Lady Patricia died in 1974 and their son, Captain Ramsay of Mar is married to the Countess of Saltoun, chief of Clan Fraser.

Queen Elizabeth the Queen Mother was born Lady Elizabeth Bowes-Lyon, fourth daughter and ninth child of the 14th Earl of Strathmore and Kinghorne, head of one of Scotland's oldest families. She was born at her parent's Hertfordshire home, St Paul's Walden Bury, but much of her childhood was spent at Glamis Castle, near Forfar in the County of Angus. This great, gloomy castle features in Shakespeare as the scene on MacBeth's murder of Duncan, but in reality Duncan died in battle at Torffness.

Glamis had come into the Strathmore family as a dowry at the end of the fourteenth century when King Robert II's daughter Jean married his secretary Sir John Lyon. The story goes that when Lady Elizabeth was seven years old there was a charity garden party at Glamis, and an old tinker woman read her palm and told her that when she grew up she would be Queen. 'In that case,' announced her governess, 'the laws of England will have to be changed!'

There has always been an air of intrigue about Glamis, although the arrival of the present generation has done much to cheer up the great old castle. Always present there is the story, rumour, mystery of the 'Monster'. It is said that generations ago there was born to an earl and countess of Strathmore a first son of such deformed appearance that it was immediately decided that this creature could never inherit the title and lands. A room was sealed off and the being kept there until its supposed death years later at a great age. Each eldest son, it is said, is told the true story, but even today when there can be no possibility of a 'monster' still being alive, there is enormous curiosity about the subject. There are stories of guests hanging sheets out of the windows while the Earl and Countess were out and there being one window with no hanging. Doubtless the true story may one day be told, but the highly unlikely existence of that 'monster' in the present day and adds a certain spine-shivering romance enormously appealing to the tourists who visit Glamis each summer.

As with all the old Scottish families there is a good deal more drama associated with the Strathmore's ancestry. King Malcolm II is said to have died or been murdered in or near the castle in 1034. In 1537, the unfortunate Lady Glamis was burned for witchcraft and for conspiring to murder James V. The castle was forfeited to the Crown before her innocence was proved, but then restored to her

Earl and Countess Spencer, the Princess of Wales' father and step-mother on a visit to Gleddoch House, Renfrewshire.

son, whose descendant, Patrick Lyon, became 1st Earl of Strathmore in 1677. In 1717 the Old Pretender stayed at Glamis and held Court, such as it was. It was here, in 1930, that the Duchess of York gave birth to Princess Margaret Rose.

The Earldom of Strathmore and Kinghorne was inherited from his cousin by Fergus Michael Claude Bowes-Lyon, the Queen Mother's nephew, son of her fifth brother. He is married to a member of the McCorquodale family and therefore a relative of the romantic novelist Barbara Cartland, who is also the Princess of Wales's step-grandmother, and they have one son and two daughters, one called Lady Elizabeth Bowes-Lyon.

The most recent Royal 'in-laws' are the Spencers and Shand-Kydds. When the Princess of Wales's parents separated, Earl Spencer remarried the colourful Raine, Countess of Dartmouth, Barbara Cartland's daughter, who has proved a stalwart second wife, helping the Earl through a recent illness and running the family estate at Althorpe. The Princess's mother remarried to Peter Shand-Kydd, who owns land in Australia and who lives on the Isle of Seil, near Oban, where he runs a beef farm. Frances Shand-Kydd until recently owned a toy shop in Oban called Menzies, which has misled more than one newspaper reporter into writing that she was the manageress of a well-known Scottish stationers.

Chapter Eight

THE QUEEN IN SCOTLAND

THE GROUNDS of Balmoral Castle are open to the public during May, June and July, daily (except Sundays) 10 a.m.-5 p.m., and there is usually an exhibition open to visitors. The Castle itself is not open for viewing as it is very much the Queen's private home and there is the obvious security risk. For the remainder of the year — August until April — Balmoral is very much a working estate. The Queen has cattle — Highland, a herd of Luing, Shorthorns crossed with Highland, and a herd of Galloways — on an estate of 35,000 acres to which she has been adding when possible. Everday affairs are managed by resident factor, Michael Leslie.

The Queen does not receive government assistance towards the running of Balmoral; it is regarded as her private inheritance, therefore not an 'official' Crown residence. She has to meet the rates bill and pay for the upkeep and maintenance out of her private funds just like any other landowner.

The Queen's staff regard the Court calendar as going from Balmoral to Balmoral, so that the year for them officially starts in Scotland. If the Royal Yacht *Britannia* is available, the Queen prefers to travel north after Cowes Week, usually through the Hebrides. This affords her considerable privacy although there is a full complement of naval staff, officers, stewards and so on. Contrary to popular belief, she is not a particularly good sailor and takes the opportunity to stay in her cabin often until after midday. Another idiosnycracy is that she likes always to have a hot water bottle in her bed, even when visiting such tropical climes as the West Indies.

By tradition, the Royal Yacht anchors for the day offshore from the Castle of Mey and the family embark by launch for lunch. The afternoon is spent enjoying the castle and grounds and the Queen Mother's hospitality and then, after tea, everybody goes back onto the yacht and it sails for Aberdeen. As the evening light dwindles on the more often than not steely grey waters, the Queen Mother

The Royal Yacht Britannia cruising in the Hebrides.

gives *Britannia* a right Royal send-off, firing huge fireworks from the battlements while her staff wave large sheets from the castle walls. In return, *Britannia* sends up answering flares. Palace staff have come to regard this rather private celebration and specatacle in the far north of Scotland as marking the end of their working year.

At one time the Royal Family would go to Balmoral from the middle of August until 20 October, but in recent years, time spent there has been curtailed by overseas visits and sudden deaths of heads of State such as President Sadat of Egypt. But no wonder the Queen enjoys her Highland retreat — it gives her as

The Queen Mother's traditional send-off for the Royal Yacht Britannia after a visit to the Castle of Mey.

Sailors on the Royal Yacht Britannia fire off flares in salute to the Queen Mother after the Royal Yacht's annual visit to the Castle of Mey.

much freedom as she is ever likely to find; bracing fresh air and privacy of a kind simply not available elsewhere, even at Sandringham.

She enjoys country life openly. She likes to walk out and about with her corgis and she likes to dress in tartan skirts, tweeds and head scarves, sensible raincoats, stout country shoes with socks or the latest vogue, Marchioness of Northampton 'wellies'. He idea of 'heaven', in fact, is a picnic, particularly when joining the male members of the family after a shoot or fishing off the Banks of the River Dee.

There is still, however, formality at Balmoral. Footmen hand round the sherry glasses on silver trays before lunch. At the two Ghillies Balls — by any standards informal family events — the Queen and the princesses wear long dresses, Stewart tartan sashes and tiaras; the princes and Duke of Edinburgh wear kilts and Highland evening jackets.

The ghillies balls are given annually for estate workers, local people and the detachment of whichever Scottish regiment is stationed at Ballater as her personal bodyguard. Scottish country dancing as danced in Scotland at parties is far from being sedate, even in the presence of the Queen. At the same time, she joins in with infectious enthusiasm, as do most of her family, and she particularly loves the Eightsome Reel and the Duke of Perth. Many people attributed the renewed popularity of Scottish country dancing at Scottish social events after the 1950s entirely to the young Queen's enthusiasm.

Each year, Jack Sinclair's band is brought in to play in the ballroom of Balmoral, starting at about 10 p.m. after dinner, and at each event the Queen makes a point of dancing with all the soldiers and many of the estate workers. It is all splendidly relaxed and enjoyable in the best Scottish tradition. Scottish reels are social dancing at its best and one of the great advantages of this kind of 'set' dancing is that everybody circulates and meets everybody else. Like her great-great grandmother, Queen Elizabeth loves the bouncy fiddle music of the Highlands.

Most days the men spend a lot of time shooting grouse, although fishing is another distraction. At night they sometimes organise barbecues, camping out in one of the tumbledown cottages on remote parts of the estate where electricity is quite unkown. Prince Philip has designed a special trailer for these occasions and this fixes to the back of a landrover so that the party can tow it over the roughest terrain. Food and drink are stored in special freezer compartments, so that the Royals can do without staff in attendance and look after themselves.

In the evening, the Queen loves party games such as 'Charades' or 'The Game', and she really does play Trivial Pursuits as is suggested by the notorious television programme *Spitting Images*. Often the family gather around the piano for a sing-song, particularly when Princess Margaret is present as she loves to sing ballads from Holywood musicals. The Queen is better known for playing Chopin or Beethoven. House guests for the first time are often appalled to find themselves asked to do comic turns after dinner. As far back as 1947, the painter Claude Muncaster recorded listening to Princess Margaret doing a Gracie Fields act and then his acute embarrassment at being asked to sing *Deep River* solo.

'Following this unfortunate anti-climax to an otherwise enjoyable evening,' he remembered, 'I was surprised to see a tartan shawl put over the firescreen; to hear that two detectives had been chosen; to find the lights suddenly turned out and the whole house party involved in a game of 'Murders'. When the last person had been murdered and the murderer discovered in the shape of Sir Alan Lascelles, it was well nigh one o'clock and everybody retired to bed.'

When the Queen has guests to stay for a weekend, she is a meticulous hostess. Although there are servants to do everything, she keeps them on their toes by checking every room herself. Guests are asked to arrive at 6 p.m. for drinks; they will be met by a lady-in-waiting or an equerry who takes them to the Queen's presence to be welcomed formally. Luggage is taken to their rooms where it is unpacked and laid out. Then, after drinks, the Queen herself escorts her guests to their rooms. Protocol is observed at all times and dinner is sharp at 8.30 p.m.

Queen Elizabeth and Prince Philip arriving at Braemar Gathering in 1952.

The Queen's greatest leisure interests are breeding horses and rearing dogs. In both areas she is considered an expert and her gun dogs are acknowledged as exceptional. One senses the priorities when at Balmoral you see a sign which reads: 'SLOW. Beware horses, dogs, and children.' There is a story that some years ago two hitch-hikers were picked up by a friendly lady in a landrover with corgis in the back seat. She looked remarkably like the Queen, thought one of the couple, but she couldn't be. Or could she? In fact, she was. But, alas, particularly since the murder of Lord Mountbatten, such situations are unlikely to occur again. In the world we now live in, even Aberdeenshire is not too far away for terrorists wanting to inflict some manic outrage.

Several years ago the Queen built a house in the woods for Prince Philip, and Lord Wilson recalls with delight being taken there for tea with his wife. They were shown around and relaxed and talked and afterwards the Queen washed up the tea things with Mrs Wilson, as she then was. Somehow it is difficult to imagine the Queen with a dish towel, but there must be moments when she positively relishes such activities.

But the Queen never completely escapes from the affairs of State, even when isolated in Upper Deeside. As in Queen Victoria's day, red and blue despatch boxes arrive overnight. Communications are more efficient than in Queen Victoria's reign, so inevitably the contents of the boxes proportionally contain more. Blue telegram boxes keep the Queen informed on foreign affairs; red boxes contain details of engagements, tours, official openings and so on. While at Balmoral in August through to October, Parliament is in recession, so she is no doubt thankful not to have to read day-to-day parliamentary reports as well.

The young Queen Victoria eulogised regularly in her diary concerning Balmoral: 'I feel a sort of reverence in going over these scenes in this most beautiful country, which I am proud to call my own, where there was such devoted loyalty to the family of my ancestors — for Stuart blood is in my veins, and I am *now* their representative, and the people are as devoted and loyal to me as they were to that unhappy race.'

Queen Victoria had also come to Scotland in her Royal Yacht, a converted man-of-war called the *Royal George*. Late August in 1842 provided the Royal progression with continual rain. They sailed up the East Coast, then travelled from Edinburgh to Perth and then to the Highlands where they were guests of the Marquis of Breadalbane at his magnificent Taymouth Castle, near Comrie. On arriving at Dunkeld, Victoria and Albert had their first encounter with the Atholl Highlanders, the Duke of Atholl's private army, armed with their Lochaber axes. She witnessed her first display of Scottish dancing and tasted whisky. At Taymouth Castle, after a great welcome, there were fireworks and in the darkness 'Welcome Victoria-Albert' was lettered out by hundreds of oil lamps and bonfires blazed from the surrounding hills. Queen Victoria was enchanted.

Prince Albert himself wrote of the experience later: 'The country is full of beauty, of a severe and grand character; perfect for the sport of all kings, and the air remarkably pure and light in comparison with what we have here. The people are more natural, and are marked by that honesty and sympathy which always distinguish the inhabitants of mountainous regions.'

Two years later the Royal couple were back in Scotland staying at Blair Castle for two weeks as guests of Lord Glenlyon. Once again the weather was unpredictable, in fact worse than the previous trip. Undeterred, the Queen announced that she was going to learn Gaelic between pony excursions into the mountains. Field sports and Highland dances were organised. Once again the visit was deemed a great success.

In 1847, the Queen leased Ardverikie from the Marquis of Abercorn. This

Queen Elizabeth, Prince Philip with Princess Anne, Prince Charles and the Queen Mother at the Braemar Gathering in 1957.

scenic shooting lodge stood on the banks of Loch Laggan which suited the Queen's quest to capture the full romance of Highland remoteness and beauty. They visited the Clyde this time, landing later at Fort William, and called in to see the Duke of Argyll at Inveraray Castle on the shores of Loch Fyne. This time the weather excelled itself. 'Alas!' confided the Queen to her diary on arrival at Ardverikie, 'the country is fine, but the weather is most dreadful.'

It looked then that the Royal couple might have had their illusions of Scottish Highland life heavily dampened. Curiously, on returning to England, the Queen's doctor reported to them with some surprise that his son, who was convalescing from an illness on Upper Deeside, reported to his father that he had experienced only blue skies and sunshine. A report was called for and confirmed

Princess Elizabeth at Ballater Station with Prince Charles held by his Nannie Miss Helen Lightbody in 1949.

that on the eastern side of the Cairngorms there tended to be comparatively little rainfall in the summer months.

In October of the same year, while taking breakfast, Sir Robert Gordon, brother of Lord Aberdeen, a bachelor with a large estate, choked on a fishbone and died. Sir Robert had earlier acquired the lease of Balmoral Castle from the Earl of Fife's Trustees, and Lord Aberdeen, to whom the estate now passed, suggested that the Queen might be interested in taking up the remaining twenty-seven years of the lease. By way of encouraging her, the landscape painter James Giles was despatched to prepare three watercolours of the castle.

Balmoral had been a fifteenth century castle, obviously built for defensive purposes and at one time owned by the Farquharson of Inverey, a branch of the Invercauld clan. After the rising of 1715, the Estate was seized by the Crown and lordship was granted to the Earl of Fife, who then made substantial alterations before purchasing the freehold towards the end of the eighteenth Century. Between 1834 and 1839, Sir John Gordon virtually demolished the original building and rebuilt Balmoral from plans drawn up by John Smith of Aberdeen.

Queen Victoria acquired the lease of Balmoral Castle on her husband's behalf in 1848. In September they set eyes for the first time on their new home, and that afternoon they walked together to the very top of the nearest hill. 'The view from here,' wrote the Queen, 'looking down upon the house, is charming. To the left you look towards the beautiful hills surrounding Loch-na-gar, and to the right, towards Ballater, to the glen (or valley) along which the Dee winds, with beautiful wooded hills, which remind us very much of Thuringerwald'.

The estate at that time consisted of 10,000 acres, to which, in 1849, the Queen added 14,000 purchased from the neighbouring Abergeldie Estate. Abergeldie Castle was acquired for the Queen's mother, the Duchess of Kent, and was later used by King Edward VII then Prince of Wales. The later purchase of Birkhall and Delnadamph in 1979 brought the estate up to 35,000 acres, but as such this is a relatively small landholding compared to a family such as the Wills, who are reputed to own 263,000 acres in Scotland.

A former member of the Royal staff described what it was like to live at Balmoral. 'Very cold outside, but comfortable and warm in the house. Most of the furnishings, and even the gold and white wallpaper with "V Rex" embossed on it, were left over from Queen Victoria's days. I doubt if the house has changed much since then.' Tartan — carpets, walls and even on the linoleum — was employed everywhere by Queen Victoria. After a stay at Balmoral, Lord Clarendon noted, 'the curtains, the furniture, the carpets . . . are all of different plaids, and the thistles in such abundance that they would rejoice the heart of a donkey'.

There are two traditions at Balmoral which Queen Victoria and Prince Albert began and which continue to this day . On the first Sunday of their annual visit, the Royal family attends the service at Crathie Church, the original replaced in

1894 by the present church. The second event is to patronise the annual Braemar Highland Games.

This particular gathering, one of the many similar local events throughout Scotland, is probably the oldest on record. It is said that King Malcolm Canmore summoned the clans to the Braes of Mar for trials of strength so that he could choose his 'hardiest soldiers and his fleetest messengers'. By the nineteenth century, these trials of strength had developed into the more formal contests such as tossing the caber, putting the shot, hill racing and tug-of-war. It is nowadays not Scotland's largest such gathering, but it is always a colourful spectacle enhanced by the Royal presence which brings tourists from all over the world.

For much of her personal style, Queen Elizabeth has taken her mother as an example. As Queen Victoria had her mother staying close by at Abergeldie, the Queen Mother has her residence today at Birkhall, situated eight miles away from the castle itself. But the Queen Mother has an independent Scottish streak and Birkhall must have melancholy memories for her of the days when she and her husband stayed there as Duke and Duchess of York.

The Castle of Mey, on the other hand, is entirely of her own creation. This sixteenth-century castle, once a Clan Sinclair stronghold, was in serious disrepair when the newly widowed Queen Mother came across it. She simply decided that it was far too beautiful with its lovely location overlooking the Pentland Firth, to be allowed to deteriorate. In deciding to save and restore Barrogill Castle to its original state and name of Castle of Mey, the Queen Mother was able to overcome some of the loneliness of widowhood and by October 1955 she was able to move in. 'It is a delight to have a home in Caithness,' she announced at Wick while receiving the Freedom of the Burgh.

It is, in fact, the only property she owns. Here she keeps a herd of Aberdeen Angus and a flock of Border Cheviot sheep, and in the late summer her house parties number up to twelve guests. There are mackerel fishing in the sea and salmon fishing inland, picnics and fun dinner parties with reels afterwards. Again the grounds of Castle of Mey are open to the public at certain times of the year, but entry to the house is exclusively by invitation.

By contrast with her Highland home, the Queen's other 'official' Scottish home, the palace of Holyroodhouse, is more austere, conjuring up memories of Mary, Queen of Scots. It is not substantial in size, but has an impressive presence at the foot of Edinburgh's Royal Mile, the length of which Queen Victoria refused to travel because of the shocking poverty of the inhabitants and dreadful disrepair into which the dwelling houses had fallen. The Royal Mile today is a fashionable street of restored houses and closes and attractive shops, connecting the Royal Palace to the ancient Castle on its rock.

The Abbey of Holyrood was founded by King David I of Scotland in 1128, but the Palace itself has come through continual additions to what was once a guest

Prince Philip's dog 'Candy' plays with his master while Prince Charles looks on in 1955.

The Royal dogs 'Sugar' and 'Candy' play with Prince Charles and Princess Anne at Balmoral in 1955.

house for the Abbey. A full survey of the palace as it existed in 1663, led to the Privy Council voting £30,000 for the repair of Holyroodhouse and Stirling Castle, which had also been a Royal residence. William Bruce, the King's surveyor general, collaborating with the King's master mason, Robert Mylne, prepared plans for the virtual rebuilding of the north, east and south sides of the main court. The existing quadrangle shape was obliged to be accepted owing to the location of the Abbey Church at the north-east and the Chancellor's Court at the south, both buildings being in use. New ranges were intended to be carefully classical, with superimposed orders of pilasters. This work was carried out but internally the plan was a muddle. The entire first floor would have been filled by badly planned sets of Royal apartments, one each for the King and Queen and the other for possibly the Duke of York.

A second, more carefully thought-out scheme was prepared for King Charles II and work began in 1671. By 1672, when the Earl of Lauderdale took up residence as Commissioner of Parliament, the north-west tower and lobby in the west range had been fitted out. By December 1674 the north range was more or less complete, the east range roofed, the south range being roofed and most of the walling on the south-west tower had been built.

But kings and queens did not come to Holyroodhouse until 1822, when King George IV arrived for a visit. Even then he slept at Dalkeith House although a bed was placed in the bedchamber of the Great Apartment and he held a levee and court in the Palace. Before he departed, the King ordered more repairs to the Palace, but influenced by the sentiment of the times and Sir Walter Scott, desired that 'Queen Mary's apartments should be preserved sacred from every alteration'.

Between 1824 and 1834 nearly £25,000 was therefore spent on repairs under the supervision of Robert Reid. Queen Victoria first visited Holyrood in 1842. During her reign, the Crown got possession of the lodging of the officers of state except for the apartment of the Duke of Hamilton. The setting of the Palace and Abbey were also brought under royal control. St Anthony's Loch was formed and lodges

Prince Philip provides the push for Prince Charles and Princess Anne during the Royal holidays at Balmoral in 1955.

Queen Elizabeth and Princess Anne adjust the bridle of the pony 'Greensleeves' at Balmoral in 1955.

built in 1855. In 1861 the forecourt to the west was tidied up, and a new guardroom and stables added to replace a brewery.

In 1906 there was a proposal to convert the Abbey Church into a Thistle Chapel, but the suggestion was rejected on the grounds that the new stonework required would destroy the value as an historical document. As a memorial to King Edward VII, the forecourt was constructed to be grander and more austere in 1920. In more recent years, stone-cleaning has taken place and the soot-grimed exterior now glows pink in the evening sun.

The Queen comes to her Palace of Holyroodhouse every summer, again continuing her father's tradition. On 24 June 1953, she arrived for the first time as Queen of Scotland and took part in the age-old Honours ceremony. Since then, every year, she has held a garden party in the grounds of Holyrood Park. In 1985, this took place the day after a charity gala extravaganza organised by the BBC and held at the Playhouse Theatre to raise funds for the 1986 Commonwealth Games. Guests at the garden party were as excited at the prospect of spotting Holywood superstar Linda Evans of *Dynasty* fame as much as they were to see the Queen. Linda Evans, herself, however confessed to be extremely nervous but 'over the moon' to meet the Queen, emphasising that the Queen's magic is rather more super than superstar.

The stay at Holyroodhouse therefore is packed with official engagements —trips to old peoples' homes, opening factories, touring towns and villages and going around Scotland generally meeting the people. Prince Philip, a keen painter himself, usually manages to look into the Royal Scottish Academy's Summer Exhibition in the Princes Street galleries and on one occasion a sharp-eyed press photographer spotted Princess Anne walking on Salisbury Crags in the early morning. But while at Holyrood the Royal Family are 'on parade'. The Queen is governing her realm from her official Scottish residence.

Arriving at the Braemar Gathering 1985.

Queen Elizabeth at a Gala evening in Edinburgh with the Scottish National Orchestra.

Captain Alwyn and Madam Farquharson of Invercauld with Prince Philip at the Braemar Gathering 1952.

Chapter Nine

THE ROYAL FAMILY

HRH PRINCE PHILIP

THE ROLE of Prince Consort must surely be one of the most daunting challenges for any man of independent spirit. And to play the part with dignity yet maintain a sense of humour, deserves nothing but respect. Prince Phillippos Schleswig-Holstein-Sonderburg-Glucksberg of Greece and Denmark, who jokes that he is a 'discredited Balkan prince of no particular merit or distinction' has certainly earned himself a lasting affection among the people over whom his wife reigns as Sovereign. He has now been enacting his role in British public life for 39 years.

From the start, the marriage was entirely suitable. The Prince met the young Princess Elizabeth when she visited Dartmouth at the age of thirteen. The young naval officer was eighteen, blonde and outstandingly good looking. King George VI wrote to his mother in 1944, 'I like Philip. He is intelligent, has a good sense of humour and thinks about things in the right way.' After the traumas of the abdication 'thinking the right way' was especially important to King George. The Greek Prince took British nationality in 1947 and became Lieutenant Philip Mountbatten, RN. Four month's later the king consented to his daughter's betrothal. On the evening of their wedding, Prince Philip was made Baron of Greenwich, Earl of Merioneth and Duke of Edinburgh.

Prince Philip's early life had been disrupted by his father's exile from Greece in 1922. His parents drifted apart; his father to France and Monte Carlo, his mother back to Greece to found the Christian Sisterhood of Martha and Mary. The Prince was therefore brought up by his grandmother, the Dowager Marchioness of Milford Haven at Kensington Palace, and he was sent to Cheam Preparatory School in Surrey. Later, in Germany, he stayed with one of his four sisters at Salem, near Lake Constance, where it was first suggested that he should be enrolled at Gordonstoun School in Scotland. His brother-in-law's father,

Queen Elizabeth, Queen Elizabeth the Queen Mother and the Prince and Princess of Wales at the Braemar Gathering in 1984.

Queen Elizabeth, Queen Elizabeth the Queen Mother and the Prince and Princess of Wales at the Braemar Gathering 1985.

Queen Elizabeth with James Gordon at the opening of the Scottish Exhibition Centre in Glasgow in 1985.

Prince Max of Baden, had helped the Jewish Kurt Hahn to establish a school run on enlightened principles at Salem. When the Nazis began their rise to power, Hahn transferred to Scotland.

'Often naughty, never nasty,' wrote Hahn of his pupil. Unprompted by anticipation of his future role as Consort, Hahn's final report said of Price Philip: 'A born leader, but will need the exacting demands of a great service to do justice to himself. His best is outstanding — his second best is not good enough.'

The exacting demands of the role of husband of the Queen cannot be underestimated. And yet, unlike Prince Albert, Philip has never been called upon to play a political role. Whereas Albert assumed the duties of the Queen's Private Secretary, communicating with her Ministers, drafting Victoria's letters and was in his lifetime 'the power behind the Queen, not the power behind the Throne', there exists nowadays an able secretariat that undertakes the sensitive daily issues of government.

Prince Philip has found his energies best employed outside the Palace. He has involved himself in education, conservation, science, medicine, sport, wildlife and industry, and has never steered away from controversy when something, in his opinion, needs to be said. He jokingly refers to his personal style as 'dontopedalogy' — the science of opening your mouth and putting your foot in it.

Prince Philip enjoys Scottish Country Dancing at a Regimental Ball.

In the years of his marriage he has established that he can be independent of thought and action without upstaging his wife. This takes considerable skill and tolerance of those who, for reasons of their own, might choose to belittle his status. Queen Victoria, writing in 1856, observed that 'while the wife of the King has the highest rank and dignity in the realm after her husband assigned to her by law, the husband of a Queen regnant is entirely ignored by law'.

Philip is clearly strong-willed and a firm influence on his family, but in public, when accompanying the Queen on official duties, he goes to great lengths to demonstrate that he is very much playing the role of Consort. He is concerned nowadays with over four hundred separate organisations, and makes on average about ninety speeches a year, all of which he writes personally. He enjoys wildlife photography, but also likes shooting as a sport. He reconciles the conflict which arises from this by pointing out that far more wildlife perishes by insecticide than the gun, but at the same time he is violently opposed to anything which might endanger the survival of a species. His arguments and attitudes are very much

Prince Philip enjoys Scottish Country Dancing at a Regimental Ball.

those of a countryman. He understands forestry and agriculture. There has been something of a renaissance, for example, at Balmoral. In 1955 he introduced Highland cattle and, in 1966, a herd of Luing cattle, shorthorns crossed with Highland. In 1972 he purchased a herd of Galloways. In order to get the best out of what is in effect a relatively small estate he has introduced the very latest methods of agricultural technology.

In 1956, Prince Philip inaugurated the Duke of Edinburgh's Award Scheme, providing a challenge for young people to reach certain standards in their activities outside their schools or jobs. Four hundred types of activities qualify for entry and the Scheme became enormously popular throughout not only the United Kingdom but, in addition, the Commonwealth. Those who are awarded the highest recognition, the gold medal, are invited to Buckingham Palace to meet the Prince.

Then there are his sporting enthusiasms. He loves to sail in racing ships. When Prince Charles and Princess Anne were teenagers he took them sailing in Scottish lochs and at one time, with the ocean-going yawl, *Bloodhound*, they made a thorough exploration of the west coast. Polo and carriage driving are other pastimes. The former, however, he gave up in 1971 after a wrist injury. The latter he took up with considerable energy as a result, and he is often to be found at

The Prince and Princess of Wales at Stornoway during their 1985 visit to the Western Isles. The Prince had not forgotten the problems of his previous visit in 1961.

Princess of Wales.

championships in Scotland such as take place at Scone Palace or at Mellerstain, near Kelso in the Borders, the home of Lord Binning. Unlike the Queen, however, he shows little interest in racing or breeding horses.

Another hobby is painting, at which he is quite accomplished. He prefers landscapes although occasionally tackles figures and still life. He is modest about his talent — 'I don't claim any exceptional interest or knowledge or ability,' he says. 'It's strictly average.' But he took lessons from the artist Edward Seago, and often visits exhibitions such as the annual Royal Scottish Academy summer show in Edinburgh. He is quite prepared to speak his mind on the subject of modern art, although is equally enthusiastic when he recognises real ability. Through a meeting in 1948 with the painter George Halliday and Gordon Russell, the Prince took steps to encourage the pursuit of good design and from this came about the Design Centre and an annual award for good design at work.

Foremost Philip is his own man, sensitive to the expectations of his role in the First Family, both public and private. 'I am not a graduate of any university,' he once told a conference of academics. 'I am not a humanist or a scientist, and oddly enough I don't regret it. I owe my allegiance to another of the world's few really great fraternities, the fraternity of the sea. At sea you will find all the conflicts that man has had to contend with now and in the past: the fear of the unknown, the power that is greater than man and his machines, the necessity to reconcile human frailties to scientific gadgets.'

The Queen's husband brings a refreshing directness to the sometimes stuffy world of the Royals. You recognise an honest man who is not afraid of blunt speaking in a world inevitably peopled by sycophants.

The Prince of Wales on a visit to Dundee.

HRH THE PRINCE OF WALES

It is an unenviable state to be born the child of a famous parent, notwithstanding the reflected glory. So very much is expected of you. But to be born famous from the start, and to be expected to fill a predestined role must be an overwhelmingly intimidating prospect.

From the moment of his birth on 14 November 1948, Prince Charles of Edinburgh was in line to succeed to the throne. His mother, Princess Elizabeth, was already heir-apparent. At three years of age he became Duke of Cornwall, Duke of Rothesay, Earl of Carrick and Baron Renfrew, Lord of the Isles and Great Steward of Scotland. The title of Prince of Wales was to be bestowed by the sovereign on his attaining the age of twenty-one. The reality of his position, he says, dawned on him slowly and it was better that way. 'Rather than someone suddenly telling you, "You must do this" and "You must do that", because of who you are.'

Times and attitudes were changing in the 1950s and 1960s, but an heir to the throne had never been sent away to school at such a young age as Charles when, at the age of thirteen, he was enrolled at Gordonstoun School in the north-east of

The Prince of Wales shows the Queen Mother her photograph on the front cover of the Braemar Gathering programme.

The Prince and Princess of Wales during their tour in 1985.

Scotland. Although it was known that Prince Philip had thrived on the lifestyle at Gordonstoun, it had not been at all a foregone conclusion that his son should follow in his footsteps. Eton was considered by many observers as being far more appropriate. To add to the speculation, the Queen and Prince Philip had undertaken a tour of possible schools which had included Fettes in Edinburgh. At the same time the Queen Mother had been describing Charles as 'A gentle boy with a very kind heart', possibly inferring that the rough, tough image of Gordonstoun might be entirely unsuitable.

In 1959, Prince Philip donated £1,000 towards the building programme at Gordonstoun. This was not seen as being a definite indication that the decision had been taken but, in due course, an announcement was made. Prince Charles's own reaction to the news and reports of the school's Spartan reputation was that it all sounded 'pretty gruesome'.

Looking back now he says that he is glad he went to a tough school, although at the time he 'hated school and hated leaving home. I was going to run away and hide in the forest.' But in the end he agrees, 'It was an education which tried to balance the physical and mental, with the emphasis on being self-reliant.' Contemporaries and current Gordonstoun pupils confirm that the regime was and is not nearly as hard as it is often publicised as being. Certainly boys are

Prince Edward

The Queen Mother and the Prince of Wales at the Braemar Gathering in 1978.

encouraged to have cold showers in the morning, but not simply for the sake of having a cold shower. After an invigorating run to wake you up, it is a refreshing experience, and the routine was very much based on trust. There was no figure with a big stick forcing the practice, but you followed the others' example. To this day the Prince confirms that he always takes a cold shower after a hot shower. 'It happens to be most invigorating and makes me feel better.'

It is true that when the young Prince paid his first visit to the school where he would spend the following three years, he found bare floorboards in the dormitories and hard wooden beds. The boys wore shorts all the year round, little protection from the bitter North Sea wind which whips across the flat Morayshire countryside. At Windmill Lodge where he was quartered, he shared accommodation with fifty-nine other boys and was expected to make his own bed and to clean his shoes each morning. A contemporary, having first left Gordonstoun, confided to a Sunday newspaper at the time: 'Most boys tend to fight shy of friendship with Charles. The result is that he is very lonely. It is this loneliness, rather than the school's toughness, which must be hardest on him.'

There were, however, diversions outside the school curriculum. He was invited to shoot with Captain Ian Tennant, chairman of Gordonstoun's board of

The Prince and Princess of Wales at Braemar 1985.

governors, Lord Lieutenant of Morayshire and husband of the 12th Earl of Airlie's daughter. Other invitations came from Lieutenant-Colonel Kenneth Mackessack, a local landowner, and often the Queen Mother would be not far away at Birkhall on a fishing trip. She was undoubtedly sympathetic to her grandson's homesickness, but looked on his difficulties as being a training for his future life. Above all one should do one's duty, and this had been her guiding sentiment though life.

At Gordonstoun with the Prince were Lord Mountbatten's grandson, Norton Knatchbull, and his cousin Prince Alexander of Yugoslavia, but all-male public schools being what they are, there are very specific rules relating to age-groupings and friendships, and both were older than Charles. The Prince found solace in sailing and swimming, receiving his life-saving proficiency certificate.

Prince Edward, Queen Elizabeth, Prince Philip, Princess Anne and Prince Andrew with Peter and Zara Phillips relaxing on board the Royal Yacht Britannia cruising in the Hebrides.

Princess Anne

Probably the event he would most like to forget in his school career came about when, at the age of fourteen, he found himself ashore on Stornoway on the Isle of Lewis. It was to prove an early lesson in the pressures on Royal life, but it had started out as an expedition on the school yacht *Pinta*.

Stornoway is a small community and the Prince's arrival attracted a large crowd around the Crown Hotel, where the five schoolboys had been left by Charles's detective, Donald Green, while he walked over to the local cinema to arrange for an evening excursion. Although used to crowd attention, Charles found this particular invasion of his privacy relatively unbearable and took refuge in the hotel bar where, without thinking about his actions, he ordered a cherry brandy. He was, of course, under age.

It is doubtful as to whether the heir to the throne had ever been in a public bar before, let alone bought his own drink in a public place. The result was that he was spotted by a young freelance lady journalist and the next day the Prince's tippling was on the front pages of newspapers around the world, supplanting even reportage on the Profumo crisis. Even when he was reminded of the business when visiting Lewis in 1985 with the Princess of Wales, it was discernible that the Prince still finds the matter rankling. In the event, his detective was 'carpeted' and later resigned. Prince Charles was summoned to see the Headmaster, Mr Robert Chew, and as punishment was deprived of his membership of the Junior Training Plan, something he bitterly resented.

The Prince and Princess of Wales in Aberdeen on their way to a Regimental Ball held by the Gordon Highlanders.

Accompanied by Sir Kenneth Alexander, Chairman of the Highlands and Islands Development Board, and Col A M Gilmour, Lord Lieutenant of the County of Sutherland, the Prince of Wales visits Lochinver.

The major publicity surrounding such a trivial incident was indictive of what can happen if a Royal so much as scratches a nose in public. Later school exercise books were to disappear from the classroom, reappearing in the pages of Fleet Street publications. The Prince was learning that he was public property.

The years passed and Charles acquired a musical affinity, first playing the piano and then the trumpet, taking part in concerts held at Elgin and at St Giles Cathedral, Edinburgh. Later he began to learn the cello. In 1965 he took the part of Shakespeare's MacBeth in the Christmas play, an interesting role for a descendant of Banquo and King James VI & I, for whom the play had been written. Thirty years before at Gordonstoun, Charles's father had played the role of Donalbain, King Duncan's brother.

In 1966 Prince Charles was despatched to Australia for a year at 'Geelong' School, often described as 'the Eton of Australia'. His time was spent at Geelong's outpost, Timbertop, 200 miles to the north of Melbourne where a life of rural self-sufficiency and broad freedom both complemented and contrasted with Gordonstoun. He describes the period as 'the most wonderful experience of my life', taking to the Australians' directness and lack of sycophancy.

Prince and Princess of Wales on their 1985 Tour.

Back at Gordonstoun for his last year, Charles was elected 'Helper' or Head of House and the following term he was made Guardian or Head Boy. He sat his A-levels, qualifying for a University place, and his final months were spent in practising Mozart on the cello. 'I did not enjoy school as much as I might have,' he later admitted. 'But that was because I am happier at home than anywhere else. But Gordonstoun developed my will-power and self-control, helped me to discipline myself, and I think that discipline, not in the sense of making you bath in cold water, but in the Latin sense — giving shape and form and tidiness to your life — is the most important thing your education can do.'

The Prince left Gordonstoun for Trinity College, Cambridge, with a period at Aberystwyth to learn the Welsh language in preparation for his investiture as Prince of Wales in 1969. He won a BA honours degree and, on 8 March 1971, flew himself to enlist as a graduate entrant at RAF Cranwell. He was to spend the next five years in the Services.

Although the RAF, followed by Navy life, first at Royal Naval College, Dartmouth, and then on various vessels, gave him a certain anonymity and opportunity to move around largely unrecognised, this in itself created problems. When he was Captain of the minesweeper *Bronnington*, based at Rosyth, over the Forth Road Bridge from Edinburgh, he decided to throw a small party on board.

The Countess of Strathmore prepared a list of suitable girls in the immediate area and the Prince decided to make a few telephone calls himself. Under usual circumstances it is customary for an equerry to make a preliminary call, but on board ship things are different.

One of the girls on her list was having a small dinner party herself when the telephone rang. After a short absence, she returned to the table looking annoyed and one of her guests asked, 'Who was that?' 'Oh, just some joker saying he was the Prince of Wales,' she snapped. 'I soon told him where to go!'

Social life aside, the Services provided the Prince with the opportunity for adventure which he so much relishes. He enjoys trying new challenges which others might find spine-chilling — like diving under the Arctic ice. 'It was a fascinating and rewarding experience and I would never have forgiven myself if I had shirked the opportunity to dive. I think the appeal is basically to conquer one's fear of the unknown. There is enormous satisfaction in achieving something which is potentially hazardous and which requires concentration and self-discipline.' Fundamentally the Gordonstoun boy speaking. Self-reliant, attracted by the element of danger incurred in sport, the heir to the throne is an action man, who believes in being fit and healthy. Friends and members of his staff who have been with him on a stalk often express amazement at how he strides ahead, plunging deep into the Scottish moorland.

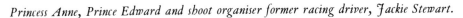

Princess Anne, Prince Edward and shoot organiser former racing driver, Jackie Stewart.

At Balmoral in the autumn he shoots grouse on average three days a week, following the tradition of his grandfather and great grandfather. His favourite equestrian pastime is polo, which he often plays at Scone in Perthshire and occasionally at Dalmahoy, the Earl of Morton's estate in Midlothian. The Queen Mother taught him the joys of angling when he was a child on the River Dee. He is both an able and enthusiastic fisherman and in the summer of 1976 he landed seven salmon on a day when the river was thought by others too low to be worth the effort. He often fishes on Loch Moore in the West Highlands, part of Anne, Duchess of Westminster's estate, and the pastime generally is one which enables him completely to escape from the pressures of his position.

He has above all a deep love of Balmoral. Of Queen Victoria he once remarked, 'She hated leaving, much as I hate leaving this marvellous place.' Such was the inspiration afforded him by Upper Deeside that he wrote a children's story to amuse his younger brothers — *The Old Man of Loch-na-gar* — which was later published with great success in aid of charity.

The Prince of Wales in his uniform as Colonel-in-Chief of the Gordon Highlanders. At the foot of the steps on the left is the late Lord Lyon King of Arms, Sir James Menteith-Grant and the Queen's Banner Bearers, the Earl of Dundee and the Earl of Lauderdale.

There had been a succession of girlfriends in the life of the Prince, most of them relentlessly pursued by the popular Press rather than by him. In 1980, however, a new figure appeared at Balmoral to spark off a certain amount of speculation among the more religious Royalty watchers. This one seemed adept at avoiding the cameras and even when confronted seemed cheerfully able to field questions with humour and casual indifference.

In September Lady Diana Spencer had been a guest at Balmoral — not particularly surprising as Earl Spencer had been a Royal equerry to the Queen in her Coronation year and her grandmother, Ruth, Lady Fermoy, is a lady-in-waiting to the Queen Mother. Besides, her middle sister, wife of the Queen's assistant private secretary, Robert Fellowes, was requiring help with her newborn daughter. There was nothing remarkable about the youngest Spencer sister being included in a large Balmoral house party.

What prompted some comment was that a month later Lady Diana was staying at Birkhall with the Queen Mother. Again hardly suggestive, as Ruth, Lady Fermoy, was also a guest. While the Prince was out and about stalking, the ladies remained indoors and worked at needlepoint. Hardly the setting for a great romance, or was it? The rest, of course, is history.

And how do they feel now? Royalty rarely gets a chance to answer back but, four years into marriage, in a television interview with Sir Alistair Burnett the couple were shyly frank about their lives. 'No,' admits the Princess of Wales, 'I didn't know what I was taking on. There were so many people watching me.' Yes, she does spend a lot of time listening to her Walkman. Why shouldn't she? Most girls of her age and considerably older like pop music. She likes Wham!, but that doesn't mean that she doesn't also enjoy Greig, Rachmananov and Schuman. And, yes, she also plays the piano, swims once or twice a day and likes to tap dance. It is nothing to get excited about.

The trivia of popular press reportage often amazes them. 'When I came on the scene I could do no wrong,' admits the Princess. 'Now its interesting to see the niggly things I'm supposed to do.'

'The media imply that I'm eccentric, for instance,' says the Prince of Wales. 'And I think I'm becoming more eccentric every day'. (This with a grin.) 'I do prefer to eat fish, but that doesn't mean that I don't eat meat. I'm not strictly a vegetarian. It seems odd to me that if you eat just meat, nobody thinks it at all odd, but if you eat just vegetables than all Hell lets loose . . . The same goes for my interest in spiritualism or mysticism. I find it rivetting what people say. It all stems from my happening to be an admirer of Arthur Koestler and the fact that a few years ago, when he died, he expressed a wish to endow a chair of Parapsychology. As Chancellor of the University of Wales I wrote to the Vice-Chancellor recommending that Wales took up the Chair. That is all. I'm not into the occult or dabbling in black magic. People say I spend a lot of time trying to communicate with Lord Mountbatten — it's ridiculous. I'm purely interested in being open-minded.'

But he does concede that part of his job, as he sees it, is to start controversy from time to time, as long as it is not party political. 'Certain things have to be said,' he says firmly. 'Sometimes I know I can throw a rock into a pond and watch the ripples.'

HRH PRINCESS ANNE, Mrs MARK PHILLIPS

The Queen's only daughter, not least because there is a shortage of princesses in the world, has been exposed to the international public gaze far more then she would ever have wished. Like her father, she is quite prepared to give a snappy retort when it all becomes too much. 'She can freeze at twenty paces,' comments a Royal observer.

Anne was born on 15 August 1950 at Clarence House. Early on she showed an interest in horses, an enthusiasm which continued when she attended Benenden School in Kent. After leaving school she began to train seriously and she had her first triumph at Burleigh in 1971 when she became European Champion. In the

Mark Phillips and Princess Anne.

Princess Anne with comedian, Billy Connolly.

same year she was voted Sportswoman of the Year by the Sports Writers' Association.

The Princess met her future husband, Mark Phillips, in 1968 at a party given for the equestrian team at the Mexico Olympics in 1968, when he was a reserve rider for the British three-day event team. Their mutual love of horses brought them closer together and they began to be seen in each other's company in public, often at horse events, such as the Dumfriesshire County Horse Trials and the member's dance in the evening at a country house near by. Their engagement was announced when the family were assembled at Balmoral and the wedding took place at Westminster Abbey in November 1973. They have a son and a daughter.

In Princess Anne's opinion, life for a princess is not at all easy, despite the advantages of her birth. 'No-one ever thought I was going to be in the least successful,' she says. 'Yes, I'm competitive. What's wrong with that? When I go into a competition I want to prove that I can be as good as anybody else.'

Although she and her husband have to a great extent managed recently to distance themselves from the glare of publicity which followed them before and after their marriage, she does resent the image that she and the Princess of Wales are at odds. This is probably one of the few areas of criticism that bothers her as, like her father, she is fairly self-contained and not particularly interested in what

Princess Anne visits Menslaws, Jedburgh in 1983 on behalf of the Border Group of Riding for the Disabled Association.

Captain Mark Phillips at a Celebrity Challenge Clay Pigeon shoot organised by former racing driver Jackie Stewart.

people who do not know her say. But of course privacy is always the problem. 'In Russia,' she reflects, 'we could go anywhere in total anonymity. But everywhere else it's a problem. We enjoyed America, but always in someone's private house or garden. They were very generous — or, to use an old-fashioned word, discreet. I don't think either of us would make good conventional holidaymakers.'

Things are easier now that the Princess of Wales attracts much of the limelight. Anne did object however when in 1982, after the intruder had been found in the Queen's bedroom at Buckingham Palace and her mother asked her to accompany her to Balmoral, the rumours started that she and Mark Phillips were separating.

The Queen helped the couple to buy Gatcombe Park, 730 acres and 600 more acres of farm, and consequently, because they live very much in the country, less attention is paid to them now, enabling them to lead relatively normal farming family lives. Although the Princess continues to helicopter around the country on Save the Children or Riding for the Disabled business or other engagements, she can often be found driving a tractor or mucking out the stables.

HRH PRINCE ANDREW AND HRH PRINCE EDWARD

Both Prince Andrew and Prince Edward followed in their brother's footsteps to Gordonstoun. Prince Andrew was born in 1960 and Prince Edward in 1964. Interestingly, the year before Andrew arrived at the Spartan educational establishment where the flat land of Moray meets the Firth, Gordonstoun had gone co-educational. His jocular comments on the subject coupled with his good

Prince Andrew, Prince Edward and Queen Elizabeth with Mr Michael Mavor, headmaster of Gordonstoun School in 1984.

looks sparked off his reputation for being something, if not more than something, of a ladies' man: 'They were a great bunch of girls. They were the frontier ladies of Gordonstoun, much the same as they were in the gold rush, and they came up and had a go.'

Prince Andrew was sent to Lakefield College in Ontario, to Dartmouth and was commissioned as a midshipman. He served through the Falklands campaign aboard the aircraft carrier *Invincible*. On his return from the Falklands he found himself pursued by the press concerning his relationship with an actress called Koo Stark whom he took to stay with the Duke and Duchess of Roxburghe at Floors Castle, Kelso, the country house setting for the recent film *Greystoke*, based on the true story of Tarzan. Since then, as the Queen's second son, his private life has continually been public gossip, the women in his life given as much attention by the public as those who were seen in the company of the Prince of Wales prior to his marriage.

Prince Edward comes over as more retiring than his older brothers. But he claims to have loved the life at Gordonstoun. 'Everybody thinks I was a proper little goody-goody, but they don't really know, do they?' One brother had gone to Australia; the other to Canada. Prince Edward went to Wanganui Collegiate, New Zealand, to teach as a junior housemaster. He is currently in the Royal Marines, having joined under the university cadet entrance scheme at

The Prince and Princess of Wales.

Princess Anne assists her husband at the Charity shoot.

Cambridge, where he entered Jesus College in 1983 to read Archaeology and Anthropology before switching to History. He likes acting and playing rugby. At a charity clay pigeon shoot held at Gleneagles Hotel in Perthshire and organised by retired world champion racing driver, Jackie Stewart, he also showed himself to be no mean shot.

Edward's will possibly be the easiest role to play in the immediate Royal circle, yet he is far from lacking in ability and is probably the scholar of the family.

HRH PRINCESS MARGARET

The Queen's sister was born in August 1930 at the Queen Mother's family home, Glamis Castle. She was christened Princess Margaret Rose, the first name at the insistence of King George V, the second after her godmother, Lady Rose Levenson Gower. On her fifth birthday the playwright Sir James Barrie, who was visiting Glamis, pointed at a present and asked her, 'Is that really your very own?' 'It's yours and mine,' she replied, delighting the old man, who used her words in his play *The Boy David*, and promised her Royalties as a result.

Throughout her life Princess Margaret has shown herself to be non-conformist although a stickler for protocol. She loves the company of glamorous international people — Rudolph Nureyev, Mick Jagger and Carolina Herrerra —in that she is drawn to the arts, enjoys ballet and show business. Few can blame her for the early disillusionment brought on by her being prevented from marrying Group Captain Peter Townsend, a handsome and much decorated fighter pilot, sixteen years her senior, who had become Master of the Household to King George VI, but was also a divorcee. Ironically, her later marriage to Antony Armstrong Jones, afterwards Earl of Snowdon, was also to end in divorce.

The Snowdons had two children and their separation has remained amiable. Since then the Princess has busied herself with Royal duties, holidaying on the island of Mustique where she has a home given to her as a present by Lord Glenconner, whose 300-roomed Peeblesshire home, the Glen at Innerleithen, was for a time also a place of refuge and privacy.

One of the Princess's great delights is to mimic and to entertain. She plays the piano and sings. At a charity fashion extravaganza and ball at Hopetoun House, South Queensferry, the home of the Marquess and Marchioness of Linlithgow, the late broadcaster, Reginald Bosanquet, somewhat the worse for alcoholic intake, made what were considered rather improper comments to her from across the table where he was seated. After a time she decided that her best recourse was to retire to her private room where, to the immense enjoyment of those present, she spent the rest of the evening rendering devastatingly witty impersonations of the unfortunate Mr Bosanquet who was not granted admission.

Princess Margaret in 1951 at Braemar. On her left is the young Duke of Kent.

Hers has not been the easiest or happiest of lives, despite the fairy-tale images of her youth. She has always had to stand in the shadow of her sister, although her own personality has shone bright and captured many hearts. Her interests are not those generally expected from ladies of her background, but then for many of her generation Princess Margaret symbolised the new, free-thinking modern woman. It must sometimes seem bitterly ironic to her that whereas other members of the family nowadays are able to marry more or less whom they please, her own early happiness was denied by protocol.

It is reassuring, however, that despite her being a stickler for formality in the way people conduct themselves towards her, she retains a wicked sense of humour and love of beauty and creativity behind the quicksilver tongue and sharp mind. In her fifties she has begun to show a strong physical likeness to Queen Victoria, being of much the same build. And she seems more relaxed, more outwardly content.

Princess Margaret at Drumlanrig Castle, Dumfriesshire. On the right is the Duchess of Buccleuch.

The young Princess Margaret attends a Civic Ceremony in George Square, Glasgow.

THE KENTS AND GLOUCESTERS

The Queen's cousins have not escaped employment in 'The Firm'. The Duke of Kent, eldest son of Prince George, Duke of Kent, and Princess Marina, was born in 1935 and succeeded to the dukedom at the age of six when his father was killed in a wartime air crash in the north of Scotland *en route* for Iceland. The young Duke suffered from bad sinus problems, so was sent to La Rosey in Switzerland. He then attended Sandhurst, after which he was commissioned in the Royal Scots Greys, a regiment which was later amalgamated to become the Royal Scots Dragoon Guards. He retired from the Regular Army in 1976 as Lieutenant-Colonel. In 1961 he married Katherine Worsley, the daughter of a Yorkshire landowner and they have three children.

The Duke's brother, Prince Michael, was born in 1942 on 4 July and because of this President Roosevelt agreed to be a godfather. He was educated at Eton and Sandhurst and commissioned in the 11th Hussars (Prince of Wales' Own). In 1978 he married Baroness Marie Christine von Reibnitz and they have two children. Prince and Princess Michael, incidentally, are not funded out of the Civil List. Prince Michael has recently grown a beard which gives him a startling likeness to his grandfather King George V.His interests, of late, have moved towards supporting the Arts and he was guest of honour when the Smithsonion Collection was on display at the 1984 Edinburgh Festival.

Princess Alexandra, Prince George and Princess Marina's daughter, was born on Christmas Day 1936. An attractive and lively personality and considered a great beauty like her mother, she married the Hon Angus James Bruce Ogilvy, second son of the 12th Earl of Airlie, whose ancestor long ago was Gillibride, second son of Ghillechriost, Mormaer of Angus. They have two children and live in London.

In 1935, King George V's youngest son became betrothed to Lady Alice Montague-Douglas-Scott, third daughter of the 7th Duke of Buccleuch and Queensberry, certainly one of the richest landowners in the United Kingdom. The family owned Boughton in Northamptonshire; Dalkeith Palace on the outskirts of Edinburgh; Drumlanrig, a fairy-tale castle in Dumfriesshire; Bowhill, near Selkirk in the Borders, and Montagu House, since demolished, in London. The Buccleuch family descend from Ann, Duchess of Buccleuch, who was allowed

A young Duke of Kent and Princess Alexandra arrive at Ballater Station.

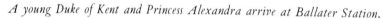

Prince Michael of Kent, Lord Binning and Princess Michael of Kent at a meet of the Duke of Buccleuch's Foxhounds held at Bowhill, Selkirk. Prince Michael has found himself some rather unusual Culottes.

to keep that title after the execution for treason of her husband James, Duke of Monmouth, natural son of King Charles II.

The Gloucesters had two children, but tragically, in 1972, two years before the Duke's own death, their eldest son, Prince William, was killed in a flying accident. The present Duke had married Birgitte van Deurs, daughter of a Danish lawyer, and had qualified as an architect when he inherited his father's title and duties. He and his family live in Northamptonshire and he is probably the only member of the Royal Family to involve himself in politics, not relating to dogma however, but in that his maiden speech in the House of Lords was a fervent attack on smoking and tobacco.

Chapter Ten

ATTITUDES AND ADULATION

AS WE HAVE seen there is a strong tradition of Royalty in Scottish life. The absence of a physical Royal presence in Scotland for over 200 years did not distance the monarchy in the national affection; indeed, when King George IV made his visit in 1822, the population was filled with curiosity, excitement and adulation of a kind, almost embarrassing to contemplate. The Scots feeling for their Sovereign is very deep-rooted in the national conciousness, whereas their attitudes towards the other 'Estates' — the Church and the Government — are regularly in conflict. The Scots are by nature an argumentative, independent race, but, as I have discussed elsewhere, they require the stability of a figure at the top, even if that figure is located for a great deal of the time in England.

Where then do Jacobite sympathies, if indeed they still exist, lie nowadays? From time to time some crank in America will announce that he descends from Bonnie Prince Charlie or from his brother, the self-styled King Henry IX, King of Great Britain. Nothing is ever surprising, but offspring of this latter gentleman could hardly be counted legitimate as he was a Cardinal of the Church of Rome, and therefore supposedly celibate. After the Cardinal King's death in 1807 in Rome, the Hanoverians had no further fears that their rights to the British throne could be challenged. They had come through several generations from King George I who had not been able to speak a word of English when he arrived to take over his Realm. Their popularity, which rose and fell with great regularity depending on the mental state of the throne's incumbent, had found a happy balance and they were generally accepted and supported by their people.

Yet Jacobitism did not die with the Cardinal King. In the century which followed, glasses were regularly raised to 'The King ower the Water', and by searching back to King Charles I's daughter, Henrietta, Duchess of Orleans, Charles II's beloved sister, Minette, and through her descendant's marriages into the Royal Houses of Europe — Savoy (Sardinia), the Estes of Modena and the

Princess Alice, Duchess of Gloucester presenting the Ladies Centenary Cup at the Melrose Centenary Seven-a-side Rugby Tournament in 1980.

Wittelsbachs of Bavaria — the Jacobites today identify their present claimant as the Duke of Bavaria, although it seems highly implausible that the present title-holder would ever consider pressing such a claim, and there is no likelihood of it ever being taken seriously.

But curious as it might seem there are some who still do uphold such a claim as an alternative to the status quo, which is interesting for it means that although they do not support the present monarchy as such, they cannot think of removing it without a similar suitable replacement. And while on the subject perhaps one should mention in passing another obscure descendant of the Stuarts, the Chevalier de Roehanstart, natural son of the Prince de Rohan and Bonnie Prince Charlie's daughter, the Duchess of Albany. Before his death Charles Edward had legitimised his daughter with the King of France's ratification. The Chevalier himself made no secret of his birthright and after a colourful life as a mercenary in the Austrian Army, in which he became a general, he died without family in Perthshire, the result of a carriage accident in 1854. He is buried in Dunkeld Cathedral, the last of the direct Stuart line, a curious reminder of a strange chapter in Scottish history. The Stuarts were never without style.

So today any challenge that comes forward to the continuance of the Royal Family comes from the people they serve — for that is how the Royal Family see their job, as servants of the people. But people are fickle and fashions and allegiances can change overnight.

Never before has so much exposure been given to Royal individuals and one wonders how Queen Victoria might have coped with television cameras. Too much exposure we must accept can be as dangerous as too little. The British have a Royal obsession, although quite different from the vocal fascination shown by the Americans. It is taken for granted that the Royals are there. We do not fawn on them. In fact, they are viewed not so much with awe as with a healthy respect providing they come up to standard, which thankfully they invariably do. We are as much at liberty to criticise as to admire and it gives the country great pride when things are so obviously going well. To be proud of the monarchy is to be proud of the country, and although the British pretend not to be jingoistic in the latter half of the twentieth century, it would be foolish to suggest that anybody would want to be ashamed of their native land.

There is no jealousy involved — in general that tends to be reserved for the tycoons of business and identifiable millionaires who flaunt their wealth. Unlike America, the showiness of wealth is considered vulgar whereas the presence of wealth is accepted providing it is accompanied by a proper sense of nobility. Does that sound pompous or trite? It is not intended to. It is simply that heritage encourages such expectations of the personages who influence our way of life. The Scots, the English, the Welsh and the Irish all have their individual brands of snobbery. It is not at all that the survival of our Royal Family or fifteen hundred years of history makes us feel superior, it is much more a sense of genuine pride in achieving continuity throughout the centuries. We are fortunate that the last time the British Isles suffered successful invasion was over nine hundred years ago, and even then the effects did not really touch Scotland, which when faced with English invasion almost three hundred years later, rallied under a monarch to triumph at Bannockburn.

We have seen the response to the Queen's Silver Jubilee in 1977, to the Royal Wedding in 1981, to the Queen Mother's eighty-fifth birthday celebration in 1985. Any observer can judge that the British Royal Family has never been more popular. But this cannot have come about without excellent stage management and remarkable commitment from the star figures.

As I have pointed out in Chapter One, the successful transition from ruling to a reigning monarchy began with King George V. Despite the setback of the abdication crisis, 'The Firm' has kept admirably abreast of the times, even setting the pace. Of course, they do have the best advisers, but it has to be more than that. An inbred instinct, perhaps? It would be good to think so, although some might disagree.

The Duchess of Gloucester with her sons Prince William and Prince Edward photographed at Drumlanrig Castle, Dumfriesshire in 1947.

Where Scotland is concerned, one cannot ignore the influence of the Queen Mother over her husband and daughter. I make no excuse for pushing the Scottish theme throughout this book because I believe it significant. Although at the time of the Coronation there was an outcry against the Queen being known as Elizabeth II in a realm where no Elizabeth I had ever reigned, this challenge seems to have become muted. Strictly speaking, she is Queen Elizabeth II *and* I as far as nationalistic Scots are concerned and it is understandable that there would be objection to ER II being stamped on letter boxes, but really these things have to be laid at the government's door and not at the Queen's.

The other bone of contention for many Scots is the presence of the Stone of Destiny under the Coronation chair at Westminster. Known as the *Lia-fail*, it was said that this was the stone upon which Jacob rested his head the night he struggled with the Angel at Bethel. It had travelled via Spain to Ireland and then to Dalriada and Scone where, for 800 years, every king of Scots was crowned upon it at Moot Hill, which is located in front of the site of the modern Scone Palace. In 1296, King Edward I removed it to England, having temporarily subdued the Scots. It is more than likely that the unpreposessing lump of red sandstone which today sits under the throne at Westminster was replaced by the Abbot of the day and the original hidden. The truth will probably never be known and geologists are reluctant to establish that this legendary accessory to kingship is a fake. The outrage which followed its removal to Scotland by a group of Scottish Nationalists in the 1950s underlined how deep feelings ran on the subject. Logically though, given that it is indeed the real thing, it does not matter where the stone is located as long as the monarch of Scotland is crowned upon it.

Opening of the Treasures of the Smithsonian Exhibition by Prince Michael of Kent during the 1984 Edinburgh Festival.

Chapter Eleven

THE QUEEN'S LOVE OF SCOTLAND

WHEN I first began my research for this book and telling people that it was to be about the Royal Family in Scotland, I was surprised at the most frequent response: 'But they don't do very much in Scotland, do they? They just take their holidays at Balmoral'. A quick telephone call to the Information Office of the Scottish Office at St Andrews House in Edinburgh tells a different story. In fact, my enquiry prompted the Press Office to put together some statistics. Royal events in Scotland in 1975 totalled fifty-five; in 1976, sixty-eight; in 1977 (Queen's Silver Jubilee year), ninety-five; 1978, sixty-six; 1979, one hundred and ten; 1980, sixty-six; 1981, fifty-six; 1982, sixty-three; 1983, seventy-seven; 1984, sixty-four and in 1985, one hundred and one. In 1985, the Queen took part in twelve Scottish events on her own; the Duke of Edinburgh, seven on his own. Together they made fourteen public appearances in Scotland. The Prince of Wales made thirteen public appearances in Scotland on his own; the Princess of Wales, four on her own. Together they attended twenty Scottish public events. Princess Anne took part in seventeen visits; the Queen Mother, six, and Princess Margaret, eight.

Most of these Scottish visits were connected with charitable causes. In 1985, for example, the Queen and Prince Philip visited Whitefoord House, the naval, military and air force veterans' residence of which Princess Alice, Duchess of Gloucester is Patron-in-Chief. They visited the Royal Scottish Geographical Society, Queensberry House, a hospital in Edinburgh's Royal Mile, Fairmile Nursing Home at which the Queen unveiled a plaque to commemorate the 50th anniversary of the death of Marie Curie and they visited the British Legion Housing Association at Eyemouth in Berwickshire. Highlight of their Scottish calendar for 1985, however, was almost certainly the official opening of the impressive £36 million Scottish Exhibition and Conference Centre beside the Clydeside Expressway, Glasgow. Equally without doubt, the event which aroused the greatest public interest in Scotland in 1985 was the Prince and Princess of Wales' visit to the Western Isles, particularly appropriate as they also hold the titles of Lord and Lady of the Isles.

The Royal Family's involvement with charitable causes is considerable and is what motivates the large proportion of their activities. Royal patronage is invaluable to organisations throughout the United Kingdom for those who seek public approbation and sponsorship for a worthy cause. To have a Royal patron is to have a seal of approval from the top. If a fund-raising event is being organised, a Royal appearance is a virtual guarantee of a sell-out, and this is the only area where the Royals could be said to be commercial, showing their crowd-pulling powers to best effect to make money.

But, of course, it would be impossible to be involved with every charity which approaches them. If they do agree to be associated with an organisation, it is because they intend to pull their weight. Any such commitment is well considered and researched in detail before a decision is made. Patronage is demanding. It is not just a question of permitting your name to appear at the head of some fancy notepaper. The Royals take their duties seriously and with so many requests for their time, their lives have to be organised with military precision. Princess Anne's work as President of the Save the Children Fund is by any standards impressive. She still found time in 1985 to visit the Scottish Council for Spastics and Riding for the Disabled at the Drum, Edinburgh, home of Mr and Mrs Allan More Nisbet. As other examples the Prince of Wales is active as President in the United Kingdom of the Abbeyfield Society and regularly visits their Scottish old people's homes, and Princess Margaret is President of the Royal Scottish Society for the Prevention of Cruelty to Children.

Then, in addition, there are military commitments in the Scottish Division. The Queen is Colonel-in-Chief of the Argyll & Sutherland Highlanders who have their Regimental Headquarters at Stirling Castle. The Duke of Edinburgh is Colonel-in-Chief of the Queen's Own Highlanders. The Queen Mother is Colonel-in-Chief of the Black Watch. The Prince of Wales is Colonel-in-Chief of the Gordon Highlanders. Princess Anne is Colonel-in-Chief of the Royal Scots and Princess Alice, Duchess of Gloucester, is Colonel-in-Chief of the King's Own Scottish Borderers.

Nobody in fairness can claim that the Royal Family is under-employed in their Scottish activities. And when you consider the immense amount of work and preparation involved for each occasion, you begin to appreciate the machinery which puts together this Royal Roadshow. For, as a well-known Scottish entertainer once remarked to me, 'The Royal Family is showbusiness at its most sophisticated level'.

Another famous Scottish personality, Jimmy Logan, was at Glamis with the Queen Mother for an evening of entertainment to raise funds for the Highland

Queen Elizabeth and Prince Philip visit Baxters of Fochabers in Morayshire.

Hospice. His feelings about her, he admits, are quite emotional. 'We talked about the war and the bombing in London and she admitted that of course there were moments when she had been afraid, but the King would never have left London and she would never have left the King.'

There have been many articles about Elizabeth of Glamis over the years, particularly in 1985 when she celebrated the same age as the century. But the underlying compliment to her is that she is the one who has seen to it that her daughter and family have followed the examples of her husband and her parents-in-law. To be a Royal was to accept that duty came before all things. Her supposed — in that it has never been publicly expressed — antagonism towards the Duke and Duchess of Windsor derived from their ultimate crime. The Duke betrayed his birthright. He failed to do his duty.

King George V remarked when his son's engagement to Lady Elizabeth Bowes-Lyon was announced, 'This is the only gleam of sunshine.' Later he was to write to his son from Balmoral, 'The better I know and the more I see of your dear little Scottish wife, the more charming I think she is and everyone fell in love with her here.' But the start was not auspicious for the new bride. Henry Asquith, the former Prime Minister, commented after attending a pre-wedding party at Buckingham Palace, 'The poor little bride, everyone says, is full of charm and stood in a row with the King and Queen and the bridegroom and was completely overshadowed.' Possibly this is true, but Elizabeth of Glamis was never over-shadowed again. Like Victoria, her husband's death left her desolate and there was a time when it was thought she might retreat from public life in the manner of that great Queen. But she was made of stern stuff and curiously rallied almost overnight when she started to read an anthology of poems sent to her by the poetess Dame Edith Sitwell. She wrote to her in a letter of thanks from Scotland: 'It gives me the greatest pleasure, and I took it out with me, and I started to read it, sitting by the river, and it was a day when one felt engulfed by great black clouds of unhappiness and misery, and I found a sort of peace stealing round my heart as I read such lovely poems and heavenly words . . . I found hope in George Herbert's poem:

> Who would have thought that my shrivel'd heart
> Could have recovered greenness? It was gone
> Quite under ground.

And I thought how small and selfish is sorrow. But it bangs one about until one is senseless and I can never thank you enough for giving me such a delicious book wherein I found so much beauty and hope, quite suddenly one day by the river.'

Her other solace, as we know, was the restoratation of the Castle of Mey, but

The Queen Mother visits the Royal Highland Show in the 1950s.

The Queen Mother at Glamis Castle. Beside her is the comedian Jimmy Logan.

by far her greatest energies were directed henceforth towards the full-time support of her twenty-six-year-old daughter. And to this day she has continued as a tower of strength. Although the masses tend to think of her nowadays as the gentle, elderly 'granny' figure promoted throughout the press and media, it would be less than justice to her qualities to accept her at face value. Here you have the last of the great Victorians, spontaneous and determined and utterly charming. Not for nothing is Adolph Hitler supposed to have remarked, after he had seen a newsreel of the King and Queen of England visiting Paris, that this was the most dangerous woman in Europe. I am sure she would laugh that off as a great compliment.

The Queen has much in common with her mother, although many compare her stateliness with her grandmother, Queen Mary. But like Elizabeth of Glamis she has strength of character and purpose, often disguised by the smiles and waves of official duties. She does tend to frown a lot more nowadays and has had the courage to be seen regularly wearing spectacles on great occasions — vanity is not a weakness she allows to influence practicability. Despite being small in height — she is five foot four inches tall — she is large in public stature. At grand occasions she can dazzle, but there is a no-nonsense enjoyment about clothes when visiting her stables or race meetings, a sort of British style suggestive of the Women's Rural Institutes, who are, of course, her devoted followers. In common with the majority of her subjects, they see in Queen Elizabeth's interpretation of the monarchy, the right degrees of intelligence and dignity, but as a woman, there is always a certain vulnerability. And this is what makes it so very much more intolerable when, on occasion, the monarchy, in the person of the Queen, comes under attack. Unlike a woman in politics, the Queen has succeeded in remaining immensely feminine, a statement which I suspect will brand me as being insensitively chauvinist. But I interpret this magnificent mix of personality as being the most brilliant of achievements, something special and unique and beyond imitation. And, dare I repeat myself, there is much which reminds us of Mary, Victoria and Elizabeth of Glamis — a collation of the finer qualities derived from their Scottish blood.

The Queen does not state opinions as such. The Royal Family prefer to be noncommittal on subjects which might lead to contention, but there are times when things need to be said and a few well-chosen words can have maximum impact when uttered from the top, often echoing the unspoken thoughts of the multitude. Not long ago the Prince of Wales told a group of Scottish businessmen in Edinburgh that Britain was in danger of becoming a fourth-rate nation and urged the people of Scotland in particular to change their attitudes and make a contribution themselves towards the creation of jobs and enterprise. The following day in Glasgow, the Queen spoke of Scotland as a great trading nation and she saw the Scottish Exhibition and Conference Centre as being much needed, worthy of Scotland's remarkable record both in exports and in the attractions of industries. 'It seems that Scotland is in some ways going through a new industrial revolution,' she observed. 'As your industries change, a forum is essential for the demonstration of new skills and technology and for the discussion of new ideas.' There was comment that while her son was attacking inertia, the Queen was heaping out praise. But taken in their rightful context, it can be argued that both speeches were truisms, and the kind of vocal comment entirely appropriate. On a more amusing note, it was fascinating to see how quickly Holyrood Park was cleared of rubbish after the Queen had described the litter problem in Edinburgh as a disgrace.

The Queen's birth sign is Taurus and it is in the Taurean character that they will stand against all-comers for what they believe to be right. She is, if it is any criticism, a little prim and inflexible, but that is entirely in keeping with her generation. Added to this she is also deeply religious and above all totally dedicated. Mary, Queen of Scots, was incidentally a Sagittarius; the Queen Mother, Leo.

A former colleague of mine, Alwyn James, a business and political journalist who was born in South Wales, tells the story about his parents who were walking along a back street in Cambridge when a large limousine passed them by, moving slowly and with a standard fluttering in front. The Queen Mother was driving through the town and the two spectators stopped and waved, the only people in the street. The Queen Mother waved back to them and flashed a brilliant smile. All their lives, recalls Alwyn, the mention of the Royal Family or Cambridge would inspire fond recollection of that experience from two people, the children of Welsh miners from the town of Aneurin Bevan and Michael Foot. That, says he, to the despair of Marxists and Trotskyites around the world, is what the Queen Mother, and, indeed, her daughter, Queen Elizabeth, and grandson, the Prince of Wales, are all about. The same glow of affection is felt by the English, the Welsh and the Scots. Whatever disruption takes place in the land; whatever pressures are put on individuals by succesive governments, the monarchy continues to guarantee that all will be well in the end.

And witness the latest Royal phenomenon; the shy, slightly chubby Lady Diana Spencer transformed into the willowy, lovely Princess of Wales, one of the most admired women in the world.

Queen Elizabeth at the Braemar Gathering in 1985. On her left is the Lord Lieutenant of Aberdeenshire.

Chapter Twelve

THE FUTURE

AT A DINNER party quite recently a French aristocrat, sustained by his family's vineyards in the Champagne District, observed to me, 'You have been very lucky, you British. You have had good people for your kings and queens. That is why you still have a monarchy.' While not disputing his conclusion, I would say that there is rather more involved than simply luck. True, recently we have had a succession of good people. Despite the abdication disruption, the Duke of Windsor earlier had created an excellent track record for himself as Prince of Wales. His brother's great achievements were to stabilise the country after a constitutional crisis and to steer his nation safely through the Second World War. And it has been Elizabeth who, by efficiently and compassionately getting on with the job, has truly popularised the British monarchy in the second half of the twentieth century.

What is the secret behind this achievement? How is it that this ancient, anachronistic institution has so subtly kept pace with the times; has been able to adapt in order to fulfil a concept in advance of requirement? How can the monarchy be so finely tuned to the needs and moods of the times when so often governments and politicians seem so hopelessly out of touch?

The answer is partly that the monarchy has no axe to grind. It does not depend on the electorate for regular re-confirmation of support. If the monarchy is vulnerable it is because if fails to do its duty. So far, in the reign of our present Queen, the monarchy can be seen to have renewed service well in excess of what could justly be expected.

And what of the Queen herself? This woman fulfilling an ancient destiny accompanied by all the trappings and ceremony of her forebears? Majesty demands an aura of mystery at all times. How is this achieved? Is it by a semblance

Queen Elizabeth the Queen Mother accompanied by Lord Lovat in 1952.

of effortlessly natural, and thereby uncontrived, superiority without giving offence? This, as I have observed before, is a quality entrenched within the Scottish character; not a question of adopting airs and graces.

One must observe that the Queen, like her mother, possesses a will of steel, camouflaged, yes, behind a generally approachable exterior. When she was younger she looked vulnerable, inspiring protectiveness; as the years passed, she seemed sterner. A monarch cannot be too approachable and the British themselves are not openly approachable. Only the Scots have discovered how to be universally friendly without necessarily encouraging familiarity. And that is how the Queen remains distant, yet can chat away to a Giffnock housewife as if she were an old friend of the family. An acute mind and a talent for inconsequential chit-chat when necessary are prerequisites for the job. To be aloof without appearing remote; to be impressive without being showy; to be grand without seeming superior.

When Princess Anne was once asked if she was ever nervous at having to meet so many people, she replied that of course she was. 'But you have to remember,' she added, 'that they are just as nervous of you as you are of them.'

How exactly, then, does one define the role of modern monarchy, by choice devoid of political power, if not invluence, in a highly technological, wealth-creating democracy? It is a subject which can be opinionated and analysed indefinitely, depending upon individual social background, political affiliation and intellectual conviction. Yet the remarkable verisimilitude about Queen Elizabeth is that she herself attracts very little personal antagonism from any quarter; sometimes the occasional disrespectful comic impersonation which, after all, is invariably affectionate and very much part of the British way of life. Queen Victoria was subject to a much rougher critical ride in her day; the caricatures in certain areas of the popular press were positively vicious.

The accusation that the Royal Family has removed itself into the British middle classes can be supported to some extent. But it is the middle classes who, as a rule, follow the example of the monarchy, rather than the other way round. It is the aristocracy, if anybody, who perpetuate the myths of privilege largely through the snobbery of individuals and the ownership of inherited land.

That the Royal Family is seen to be doing the 'right thing' is important to their subjects although, again, this concept is open to dismissal by some as middle class dullness. But the First Family must have a structure for others to emulate. And the fact that the First Family sets a Christian example for others to follow and it is found that the majority do choose to follow, then obviously the example set must be a popular one, and, as such, a good one, given that you have an intelligent free-thinking populace. Echoing what I have written right at the start of this book, this reign commenced as television sets were introduced into homes throughout the country. Never before had Royalty been exposed to such instant

Prince Edward with the Earl of Airlie, who has recently been appointed Lord Chamberlain.

and personal scrutiny. Members of the Royal Family found themselves becoming, in addition to the other demands on their abilities, television personalities. It behoved them therefore to behave with immense decorum and responsibility in order to protect their sacred obligation and not to let the side down.

Of course, this applies to the Commonwealth as well. At the present time, the Queen could, if she chose, take off to Australia or New Zealand or Canada and exercise her rule from one of those countries. Of course, it is a ludicrous prospect, but not entirely beyond the bounds of possibility. And as Britain seeks to become more integrated with Europe for trading and defence reasons, the suggestion is that the British monarchy is not as involved with Europe as some people might wish. There are those who consider this situation just as well but, with the prospect of a Channel Tunnel, it must be faced that the British way of life could be severely influenced in a way that it has never been as an island fortress.

It is interesting to conjecture that whereas the English are generally unpopular throughout Europe, this has never been the case with the Scots. The Auld Alliance between Scotland and France — a union which, it must be admitted, has always been celebrated by the Scots more than the French — goes back to 1296, when Robert the Bruce's predecessor, John Balliol, Scotland's puppet king, was driven by a committee of bishops, barons and earls to defy Edward I of England and form an alliance with Philip IV of France. Philip dumped the Scots when he married his daughter off to Edward's son, but the Alliance recurred on and off throughout the centuries, fuelled by the import of claret into ports such as Leith, and the inclination for Stewart kings to marry French ladies. And then, of course, the Jacobites found refuge with Louis XIV. There was also a lot of coming and going from other European countries, particularly in the Hague during the rule of Cromwell. Of course, the Stuarts married into most of the Royal Houses of Europe at some time or another.

Whereas an Englishman's home is his castle and his castle is England surrounded by the seas — a great comfort in times of possible invasion — the Scots have a strong European tradition. And in the last century the Royal Family, despite the burgeoning growth of the British Empire, also had a strong European relationship. Queen Victoria and Prince Albert were both related to most of the Royal Houses of Europe, although the 1914-1918 holocaust changed things irreprably.

It is probably within the context of Europe that the United Kingdom will have to come to terms with its future and there are those who fear that our influence and stature throughout the world will be diluted as a result to a state of impotence. Yet it is true to say that at the present time the signs are quite to the

Prince Philip, Duke of Edinburgh photographed in the uniform of Colonel-in-Chief of the Queen's Own Cameron Highlanders on the occasion of his thirty-third birthday, 10 June 1954.

contrary. Britain's stand over the Falklands invasion and the islanders' rights to British sovereignty impressed the world to the extent that Britain was not prepared to be knocked about, even in the far away South Atlantic.

Interest in the British constitution and monarchy from overseas has never been greater — witness the massive world coverage of the Royal wedding in 1980; and the immense interest when the Prince and Princess of Wales visited the 'Treasures of Britain' exhibition in Washington in 1985. It is a volatile, technological world we are living in and today, more than ever before, it is impossible to know what the future holds. There has never been a precedent for a British monarch to retire and things are very changed from the days of King Edward VII who felt thwarted and misused when his mother refused to give him greater powers to govern. In those days the Monarchy was a political power. Today it is not.

King Edward VII was sixty when he eventually inherited his mother's throne. It is conceivable that Prince Charles will have just as long to wait, for sources close to the Queen think it most unlikely that she will retire. One good reason, naturally, is to allow the Prince and Princess to enjoy their marriage and family life for as long as possible before the arduous business of state is thrust upon them. Remember that the Queen herself inherited as a young bride, and although she has achieved a stature beyond all admiration, she, of all people, realises what the job entails and the sacrifices which have to be made.

But, to reiterate, nobody can ever be certain what the future holds. One thing, however, can be said in tribute to two remarkable and strong-minded women to whom our whole united nation owes a monumental debt — the Queen Mother in her eighty-sixth year and Her Majesty the Queen in her sixtieth year. Both of them can relax in the confidence that largely as a result of their example and determination, with the Prince and Princess of Wales and their children held universally in the affections of the British people, the survival of the monarchy of Britain will last well into the twenty-first century.

BIBLIOGRAPHY

DESPITE THE urgency with which this book has been prepared, it would have been impossible without consultation with some of the many, varied and informative works already published on the Royal Family. Books consulted include:

Philip: An Informal Biography, John Basil Boothroyd, Longman 1971.

Edward VIII, Frances Donaldson, Weidenfeld & Nicolson 1974.

The Queen's Children, Edgar Donald, Arthur Barker 1978.

The Windsor Tapestry, Sir Compton Mackenzie, The Book Club 1939.

Charles, Prince of Wales, Anthony Holden, Book Club Associates 1979.

Majesty: Elizabeth II and the House of Windsor, Robert Lacey, Hutchinson 1977.

How the Queen Reigns: An Authentic Study of the Queen's Personality and Life Work, Dorothy Laird, Hodder & Stoughton 1959.

King George V: His Life and Reign, Sir Harold Nicolson, Constable 1952.

Queen Mary, James Pope-Hennessy, G Allen & Unwin 1959.

The Queen, Ann Morrow, Granada 1983.

The Country Life Book of The Silver Jubilee, Patrick Montague-Smith, Hamlyn 1977.

Princess, Robert Lacey, Hutchinson 1982.

Royal Family Album, Colour Library International.

The Way the Wind Blows, Lord Home, Collins 1976.

The Tartans of the Clans and Families of Scotland, Sir Thomas Innes of Learney, Johnston & Bacon 1938.

INDEX